Ancient History

*A Concise Overview of Ancient Egypt,
Ancient Greece, and Ancient Rome - Including
the Egyptian Mythology, the Byzantine
Empire and the Roman Republic*

Eric Brown

Table of Contents

Ancient History

Ancient Greece

Ancient Rome

Ancient Egypt

A Concise Overview of the Egyptian History and Mythology Including the Egyptian Gods, Pyramids, Kings and Queens

Additionally, the information in the following pages is intended only for informational purposes and should thus be thought of as universal.

As befitting its nature, it is presented without assurance regarding its prolonged validity or interim quality. Trademarks that are mentioned are done without written consent and can in no way be considered an endorsement from the trademark holder.

Introduction

In this book, you will find both the history and the mythology of ancient Egypt. This period of time in the Egyptian history is commonly accepted to be between the years circa 3100 B.C and 332 B.C. These are the years when the land of Egypt was united into a single kingdom and when Alexander the Great, the king of Macedonia, conquered Egypt and forced Queen Cleopatra the VII to surrender to the Roman Empire.

Whether you want to learn more about Tutankhamun, whose tomb was discovered in the year 1922 and filled with gold and riches, or Cleopatra the VII, the famed last queen of Egypt, you will have the opportunity in this book to learn all about some of the most prominent rulers of Ancient Egypt. As well as the history of the pyramids, temples, and religion, how the Nile was an integral part to survival, the Egyptian army, and battle practices, how transportation and trade affected life, the daily life of ancient Egyptians, as well as their mythology, time periods, and dynasties.

The life of the ancient Egyptians was not easy. If the water level of the Nile was only too low or high, it would cause devastation. They were isolated, yet they always have to be ready for an attack on the Pharaoh and their capital. Upper and Lower Egypt were both quite different and separated, making it more difficult to govern. Yet, in order to live prosperously, both portions of Egypt had to work synergistically. This took the effort of the Pharaoh, local governments, and the people. It was not an easy environment to live in, but by working together, the people were able to survive.

Chapter 1: The Periods of Ancient Egypt

When discussing ancient Egypt, there are many time periods that are mentioned, and these are classified by important events and the rulers of Egypt at the time. These time periods range from the very beginning of Egypt when they are forming into a single country to the dissolution of the country.

Predynastic Period: c. 5000-3100 BC.

Much is still unknown of the period prior to the unification of Egypt into a single country. Before the reign of the Pharaoh Menes, there is not much evidence of who the ruler was. The belief of ancient Egyptians was that before the rule of Menes, the land was ruled by gods and then followed by demigods.

The most common belief was that after the creation of the earth, the land of Egypt was ruled by the sun god, Amun-

Ra, and then by his heirs. Later on, it was believed that due to near constant attacks from powers of darkness and rival gods, the Pharaoh god Osiris was murdered by Set. Osiris was one of the most well-known and loved gods in Egypt and was married to his sister, Isis. He was known as the Lord of the Underworld, Judge of the Dead, the Lord of Love, Eternal Love, and King of the Living. Set was originally loved, believed to have saved the sun god Ra, and to helped people both in life and death. He was said to rule the Upper Egypt. However, this changed once he was believed to have been the first murderer, who murdered his brother out of jealousy and then tried to murder Osiris' son, Horus. From then on, Set's rule brought chaos to Egypt.

After Osiris was murdered, his son, Horus, the sky and falcon god was believed to have defeated Set and brought peace back to Egypt. After he passed away, it was said that he bequeathed his throne to humans and that the Pharaohs were reincarnations of Horus.

Not much is known of the pre-dynastic period aside from the mythology. This is because mythology was incredibly important to the ancient Egyptians' way of life, and they worked hard to preserve their beliefs. But, it is known that Menes was the first ruler of Egypt as a unified country when he united the Red Land in the Delta and the White Land in the southern kingdom. The Egyptians also began making more pottery, tools, utensils, and weapons, and largely replaced hunting with agriculture.

Though the lands were now unified as one country, they continued to be referred to as The Two Lands. The Pharaoh would wear both the Red Crown and the White Crown. Sometimes, the two crowns were combines to form the Double Crown.

Archaic Period: c.3100-2686 BC

The Archaic Period of Egypt is when Menes and his decedents developed and established many of ancient Egypt's traditions and social structure. One of his first actions as ruler was to create a new capital city in the Delta. Originally, this city was most likely known as "White Walls," but later became known as Memphis. This capital city became one of the great cities in ancient times and was the center for the royal family, the treasuries, foreign trade, judiciary hearings, and was even a well-known area for the arts.

At the temple of Hieraconpolis, also known as Nekhen, there was a slate palette called Narmer's Palette that was possibly placed there by the Pharaoh Menes in order to give thanks to the gods for his victory in unifying Egypt. This large palette, which can be found at the Egyptian Museum in Cairo, commemorates the unification. On the pallet, the Pharaoh is displayed wearing both the White Crown and the Red Crown as he conquers the land.

During this time, the Egyptians first began trying to preserve the bodies of the dead. They began to form structures known as a mastaba which means "eternal house" and originates from the Arabic word which means "bench". These mastabas would later on used only by commoners. However, in the early period of Egypt, they were solely used by royalty and high-ranked officials. The mastaba was made of mud from the Nile, stone or bricks. These were used to protect the body from grave robbers and animals. However, they only dug a grave and failed to properly preserve the body. Therefore, the ancient Egyptians began to experiment with mummification.

The Old Kingdom: c.2686-c.2181 BC

By the time of the Old Kingdom, the structure and society of ancient Egypt had already been established during the Archaic Period. Egypt had become an incredibly successful country with great strides in architecture, literature, technology, medicine, metalworking, masonry, and art. The Pharaoh held absolute power over Egypt, and King Cheops began to devote a great amount of the country's wealth towards building The Great Pyramid in Giza during the fourth dynasty. The building of the pyramid led to a great drain on Egypt's resources. Eventually, it led to the decline of the Old Kingdom.

While the idea of the Pharaoh being a god-king was standard throughout ancient Egypt, it was most prominent during the Old Kingdom than any other time. The kings were believed to be part god and divine, and they would erect statues in their honor. It was also believed that only the Pharaoh could attain an eternal after-life, which they would then spend sailing with the gods in heaven. The Pharaoh was surrounded by many officials, whom they would often delegate matters such as religion, politics, law, warfare, justice, and social issues. The Pharaoh would also take many wives and mistresses, which could result in many disputes over who would become the heir. In order to lessen rivalries, the king would offer wealth, land, influential positions, and lavish tombs to his relatives. Around eighty percent of the population was peasants whose opportunities and lives were limited. These people spend most of their time growing agriculture to feed the population and to submit as offerings to the tombs and pyramids, as well as irrigating the land.

When the land was flooded by the Nile for about three months of the year, the people were most likely paid to labor on the pyramids or conscripted into the military.

The first of the stone periods was built during the third dynasty and is known as Djoser's Step Pyramid at Saqqara. Afterward, the pyramid structure continued to be refined throughout the fourth dynasty, but declined during the fifth dynasty and ceased with the end of the Old Kingdom.

First Intermediate Period: c.2181-1991 BC

During the First Intermediate Period dynasty, five passed away with the decline in the pyramid construction. By the end of the sixth dynasty, both the wealth and the power of the Pharaoh were fading. After Pharaoh Pepi II died of old age after ruling for over ninety years, the sixth dynasty ended and the government collapsed. This led to chaos across the land all throughout dynasties seven to ten. However, this period of chaos passed during the eleventh dynasty when a strong ruler was crowned as Pharaoh. The time of chaos between the seventh and eleventh dynasties is what is now known as the First Intermediate Period. This collapse and chaos were caused by many factors including religious, economic, and political reasons.

There are several important phases and notable events in the First Intermittent which include:

- At the end of the sixth dynasty, the country collapsed which lead to many kings to reign for only short periods of time throughout the seventh and eight dynasties.

- The central government in Memphis dissolved, which lead to civil wars along with widespread conflict, disease, and famine. This was worsened by infiltrators by Bedouin.

- Throughout the ninth and tenth dynasties, they were able to attain a temporary state of calm and cease the civil wars due to a new line of rulers gaining control over the area of Middle Egypt (between Memphis and Thebes). This was thanks to Akhtoy, who originated as a governor over Heracleopolis and whose line led these two dynasties.

- Afterward, a family of rulers from Thebes battled with the previous ruler from Heracleopolis and won. The most powerful ruler in this family was Mentuhotep Nebhepetre, though there is little known about how he overcame the previous ruler. However, he made himself the first king of the eleventh dynasty, which led to a period of peace. Mentuhotep also made Thebes the capital and was later buried there.

Middle Kingdom: 1991-1786 BC

The eleventh dynasty most likely ended when Amenemhet, who had been the vizier to the previous king, is believed to have assassinated the king before taking the throne for himself. This was the beginning of the twelfth dynasty. During this period of time, ancient Egypt once again flourished and was ruled similarly to how it was during the Old Kingdom.

While Amenemhet's father was not of royal blood, he was able to succeed in keeping the throne in his family for a number of years by making his eldest son, Senusret I, his coregent so that they ruled together for the last twenty years of his reign. This meant that even if the Pharaoh was assassinated, the next ruler in line for the throne was already established. During this time, the capital city was also moved to It-towy, quite a distance south of Memphis.

The nobles retained many privileges at first. But, as the increase of noble privileges is part of what lead to the kingdom's downfall during the Old Kingdom, the privileges eventually decreased. In order to lessen the risk the nobles posed to the throne and the economic drain of awarding them land and wealth, Senusret III removed many of their rights. Nobles were no longer allowed to build their tombs next to that of the Pharaoh but rather, built them along the Nile River. By the end of Senusret III's reign, the nobles were replaced by a middle class that consisted largely of the farmers, craftsmen, and tradesmen.

Second Intermediate Period: 1786-1567 BC

The reign of Amenemhet III during the twelfth dynasty was highly successful, but the country was once again sent into disarray when his coregent, Amenemhet IV, and his sister Sobekneferu took the throne at the end of the dynasty. Egypt suffered many difficulties under the Second Intermediate Period, greatly due to the rapid succession of new kings and a failing government.

During this time of chaos, more specifically during the fifteenth and sixteenth dynasties, foreign leaders known as the Hyksos infiltrated Egypt and conquered it by overtaking rulership rather than by military force. While the Hyksos did overtake Egypt, it appears that they likely adopted many of Egypt's preexisting government practices, religion, and arts. The southern parts of Egypt appeared to have retained a considerable amount of autonomy from the Hyksos reign, though they were required to pay taxes.

Towards the end of the Second Intermediate Period, the tension between the native Egyptians and the Hyksos rose, and it came to an end when the native Theban rulers of the seventeenth dynasty began to battle against the Hyksos. These princes were, later on, regarded as heroes who took back Egyptian land and drove the Hyksos into Palestine before overtaking them. The three Theban princes who were most influential in this were Kamose and Seqenenre Ta'o II of the second dynasty and Amosis I who would soon establish the eighteenth dynasty.

The Hyksos incident made a lasting impact on the Egyptians which prepared them for the coming ages. The Egyptians became less isolated, and rather than solely looking to gather resources, they also wished to attain more power abroad. They began to adopt more fierce foreign policies and war tactics in order to prevent others from seizing Egypt.

The New Kingdom: 1567-1085 BC

The Theban princes who had defeated the Hyksos created their own dynasty and strengthened it by marriages through close relations. The major cities and military bases such as Memphis and Heliopolis continued to flourish, but the princes decided to retain Thebes as the new capital of Egypt.

These rulers of the eighteenth dynasty attributed their great success in leadership and in defeating the Hyksos to their local god, Amun. Amun was, originally, the God of Air. In order to prevent Amun from having any rival, the Pharaohs began to associate him with the sun god, Ra, and renamed him Amun-Ra. During the mid-eighteenth dynasty, the worship of Amun-Ra reached its peak, and he was believed to be the creator of all people.

Amun-Ra's religious center was Thebes, which soon led it to become not only the most important political city but the religious city with the most import, as well. This led to Amun-

Ra's priesthood gaining unprecedented power even over the throne. If the line of succession was in dispute or someone's claim to the throne was weak, then the priesthood would either grant or withhold Amun-Ra's blessing. At the end of the eighteenth dynasty, the Pharaoh attempted to take away some of this power from the priesthood but was unsuccessful, and they continued to play a powerful political role for dynasties to come.

During this time, the Pharaohs selected a new area for burial which is now known as the Valley of Kings. Rather than building pyramids, as was traditional, they rather decided to be buried into tombs made of deep cut rock. Supposedly, this was to prevent grave robbing which was common from the pyramids. However, this burial proved to be unsuccessful in preventing grave robbing in most cases. The only exception was the grave of Tutankhamun whose burial site was uncovered practically untouched during 1922. The Egyptian empire had a surge of success during the mid-eighteenth dynasty, due to it being the first of the world's empires. The Pharaohs successfully conquered multiple countries and were able to establish an empire all the way from Nubia (which is now partly in Egypt and partly in Sudan) to the Euphrates River (which is in Iraq).

The Pharaohs of the eighteenth dynasty were infamous for their military tactics and courage. Tuthmosis III undertook a sixteen-year conquest in order to subdue Syria and Palestine. Later on, under the rule of Amenhotep III, the royal family and the government replaced conquest and war with peaceful diplomacy through gifts and marriage arrangements.

Near the end of the eighteenth dynasty, both the political and religious sectors of Egyptian life were thrown into disarray. After inheriting the throne from Amenhotep III, King

Amenhotep IV and Queen Nefertiti began to make unprecedented changes to the customary Egyptian beliefs. The two began to build temples to their preferred god, Aten, in close proximity to the temples of Amun-Ra. Not only did they wish to elevate their preferred god, as was normal among the rulers of Egypt, but they wanted sole worship of Aten and no other deities. Amenhotep IV took this so far as to disband the priesthood of all the gods except Aten, divert a great amount of income towards the worship of Aten, wiped the other gods' names from monuments, and even changed his own name to Akhenaten (Servant of the Aten). Soon, thereafter, he built a new capital city and palace from Thebes to middle Egypt and named it Akhetaten which is now known as Amarna. While they moved the royal family, court, officials, craftsman, and many other people to Amarna along with building many palaces and tombs, the time spent there was not long. Since there was no direct male heir to the throne, the royal family was most likely pressured by senior courtiers to move back to Thebes which left Amarna deserted. After returning to Thebes, the religion went back to its traditional roots of worshiping many gods.

During the nineteenth dynasty, war and conquest once again resumed as Sethos I and Ramesses II began another war against the Hittites. However, they realized that neither side could win the war. In the twenty-first year of his reign, Ramesses II made peace with the king of the Hittites. This was soon followed by a friendship between the royal families and the marriage of Ramesses II to a Hittite princess who became Queen Maathorneferure.

During the nineteenth dynasty, King Merenptah fought off invaders from the Eastern Mediterranean region who desired to settle in the Delta. They returned once again during the nineteenth dynasty but were once again defeated, this time by Ramesses III. While Ramesses III experienced a highly successful reign, he is considered one of the last great kings of Egypt, as the ones that followed were much less successful. The twentieth dynasty ended with the death of Ramesses XI.

Third Intermediate Period: 1089-525 BC

After the New Kingdom, Egypt once again began a slow decline, known as the Third of the Intermediate Periods. This third decline took place between the twenty-first and twenty-fifth dynasties. Some periods during this time, Egypt was subjected to foreign powers ruling over them.

Once the last Pharaoh of the twentieth dynasty, Ramesses XI, passed away, the following Pharaoh, Nesbenebded, changed his name to Smendes and founded the twenty-first dynasty. During this dynasty, Smendes and his successor no longer ruled all of Egypt, but rather the Lower Egypt with their capital city being in the Delta City of Tanis. While they may have been legitimate kings, it was the priests of Amun who ruled the Middle and Upper Egypt, south of Thebes. Surprisingly, this arrangement seems to have been amicable, and there were frequent marriage arrangements between the princesses and the priests. However, the country suffered greatly from the lack of a unified and strong leadership during this time.

During this time, many mummies and the treasures they were buried with were rescued from their tombs. Due to frequent grave robberies, the high priests of Amun, Pinedjem I and Pinedjem II, who ruled the southern portion of Egypt, ordered to have many mummies from the New Kingdom to be reburied in other tombs. Many of these mummies were relocated to the tombs of Queen Inaha'pi, Amenhotep II, and into the tombs of other royalty and priests.

Dynasties twenty-two and twenty-three are known as the Libyan or Bubastite dynasties. This is because, after the end of the twenty-first dynasty, Psusennes II had no male heir, so his son-in-law who was from the Delta city of Bubastis became Pharaoh. The first Pharaoh of the twenty-second dynasty, Shoshenk was a powerful chief and commander in the army. In order to regain control of southern Egypt, he appointed his second son as the high priest of Amun.

Despite regaining the control of the whole of Egypt, the country continued to suffer. This suffering was transcribed upon the walls of the entrance of the main temple in Karnak. Yet, the Pharaohs retained enough power to afford the building of monuments and to be buried with large amounts of treasures. During this time, Thebes continued to be a religious center, while either Tanis or Bubastis was the capital.

Shortly after this, the documentation is more difficult to track. Yet, it is evident that there was some sort of breakdown in the government, as some of the kings of the twenty-second and twenty-third dynasties ruled simultaneously.

The twenty-fourth dynasty only had two rulers, Tefnakht I and Bakenranef, who ruled a limited area from Sais in the Delta. While Tefnakht attempted to gain more power towards the south, this failed due to the ruler of a kingdom far south of Egypt. This ruler, Piankhy, conquered southern portions of Egypt and subdued the northern portions before he returned to Napata, Nubia.

While Egypt continued to be ruled in various parts by different princes, Piankhy's brother, Shabako, soon returned and defeated Bakenranef in Sais. The twenty-fifth and Nubian-ruled dynasty began after choosing Thebes as the capital city. Though the building of pyramids had ended hundreds of years prior, the Nubian rulers once again began building these magnificent tombs and both Pianky and Shabako were buried in pyramids in Kurru.

Later on, King Taharka was crowned in Memphis, and while he was an effective Pharaoh, there was much conflict with the Assyrians at this time. This was because, after a request for aid, Egyptian forces fought against the Assyrians when they attempted to invade Judah, Syria, and Palestine. Due to the Egyptians getting in their way, the Assyrians became resentful and soon attacked Egypt. While they were at first unsuccessful, they attacked again a few years later which resulted in causing King Taharka to flea out of Memphis and head southwards. While the Pharaoh escaped, the Assyrian ruler stole treasures and people from the capital.

New rulers who were loyal to the Assyrian government were elected among the local Egyptian governors. Once the King of Assyria, Esarhaddon, passed away, Taharka attempted to retake his country. Yet, the new Assyrian king once again regained control of Egypt, causing Taharka to flee once again, first to Thebes and then to Napata. Taharka's nephew and heir, Tanuatamun, also attempted to regain power. However, he was also unsuccessful as the Assyrian king once again attacked and caused him to flee as well.

The Nubian kingdom, which had held power over Egypt for the twenty-fifth dynasty, eventually gave up on Egypt and continued to live within their own country's boundaries. Yet, they had adopted some of Egypt's cultures into their own and both countries continued to trade with one another.

The Late Period: 525-332 BC

The Late Period of Ancient Egypt was marked by a frequent change of leadership, especially by invaders such as the Assyrians.

Despite the Assyrian government electing Egyptian as governors during the twenty-fifth dynasty, they soon found that these Egyptians were not loyal to them as they had believed. Rather, the Egyptians changed their allegiance to the deposed Nubian rulership with both military and political support. The Assyrians fought back and restored Necho I and his son Psammetichus I from the Delta city of Sais as petty rulers. The son, Psammetichus I, became the first Pharaoh of the twenty-sixth dynasty. This dynasty was able to restore a temporary peace and power to Egypt, though it still continued to decline and the country never again was able to regain the overwhelming power it once held.

Necho I had established a small but important kingdom in the western area of the Delta, and most likely ruled as a local Pharaoh with Sais as his capital. Yet, his reign did not last long, as he was murdered by the Nubian rulership, which had briefly regained control of Egypt during the twenty-fifth dynasty.

The Nubian government was then deposed by the son of Necho I, Psammetichus I. Most likely, Psammetichus I originally only ruled the northernmost parts of Egypt, while the Nubian rulership controlled the remainder. However, Psammetichus eventually was able to take control of the entire country and reunify Egypt once again.

In order to strengthen his power, Psammetichus I, father of Necho II, continued a tradition of earlier dynasties by appointing his daughter, Nitocris, as the Divine Wife of Amun at the temple in Thebes. While during the New Kingdom this title was originally appointed to the wife of the Pharaoh and she would act as the consort of Amun in festivals, the title, later on, began to carry more political power.

The daughter of the Pharaoh would become priestess who would award her with both religious and political power, as well as riches and land. While she was not allowed to marry, she would adopt the daughter of the following Pharaoh to become her successor. This allowed there to be a smooth line of succession and gave the Pharaoh more control over Thebes and the southern portions of Egypt. Due to the Wife of Amun being unable to marry, this would also ensure that she did not have a husband or son who might try to take power from the royal family.

The twenty-sixth dynasty had been able to regain control of the throne with the help of foreign allies and military, including the Greeks, Syrians, Jews, and Carians. Due to their help, they encouraged foreigners to settle in the land of Egypt. However, this caused resentment from the local population. Therefore, they had to create cities specifically for these foreigners, and Psammetichus I created Naucratis in the Delta specifically for the Greek settlers.

Yet, due to the short time of peace, disinterest in gaining international power, and the increase of foreigners settling in the land, Egyptians expressed an increase of interest in their traditions. This led to a phase of increased artistic expression, monuments, and literature, which would remind Egyptians of their history and culture for generations.

With the reign of Necho II, son of Psammetichus I, Egypt once again became interested in the trade, exploration, and foreign affairs. This increase in foreign affairs ended in the Babylonians seeing Egyptians as an enemy and has many battles, which resulted in the Babylonians seizing all of Egypt's foreign territories.

Despite previously battling with the Babylonians, several generations later, the Egyptians and Babylonians formed an alliance together in order to hold off the rising Persian Empire. However, their alliance was to no avail, as the Persians conquered both Babylonia and Egypt, killing the last Pharaoh of the twenty-sixth dynasty in the process, King Psammetichus III.

The remaining portion the Late Period had many Pharaohs in quick succession. Egypt, at this time, was seen as a province of the Persian Empire. Therefore, Egypt was ruled by a governor or Pharaoh on behalf of and representing the King of Persia. Some of these Pharaohs in the twenty-seventh dynasty were seen in a positive light, whereas, others were seen as tyrants. Darius I was seen as a positive giver of the law who helped the people of Egypt and completed a canal which linked the Nile and the Red Sea. On the other hand, Cambyses II and Xerxes I was tyrants who struck down multiple uprisings.

Overall, while the Persian control over Egypt did affect the people, it had little impact on the Egyptian culture and way of life. Yet, the Egyptians were thankful when they were freed from the Persians by Alexander the Great.

Ptolemaic Egypt: 305-30 BC

After the ruler of Macedonia, Phillip II, was assassinated, Alexander the Great took his place on the throne with the help of his supporters. Alexander was known for his brilliant tactics and leadership. Because of this, he was able to overtake the Persian Empire and, therefore, take over the territories that the Persians had previously conquered including Egypt. Due to Alexander's quick succession in taking over new territories, he allowed them to maintain much freedom including the freedom to practice their own religion and traditions.

Alexander the Great was crowned Pharaoh by the priests of Egypt and spent six months in the country establishing the new government. He appointed a viceroy as well as six governors, two from Macedonia and two each of Greek and Egyptian origin. Garrisons were built, finances were put under a Greek system, and a new capital city, Alexandria, was built along the Nile and the Mediterranean coast. Alexandria became the new capital city, and its position ensured it would be a center of Greek knowledge and learning.

After Alexander the Great left Egypt, he died in Babylon in 323 BC after falling ill. After Alexander's death, his empire was divided amongst his generals. The Macedonian general Ptolemy, son of Lagos, who was in charge of the Egyptian troops became a leader of Egypt first under Alexander the Great's Brother and then his nephew, Alexander IV. In the year 305 BC, Ptolemy became the sole king of Egypt and took on the title Ptolemy I Soter, which means Savior.

Ptolemy I was fixated on securing his new dynasty, and his efforts were successful for nearly three centuries. To accomplish this, he claimed the title of Pharaoh; appointed his son, Ptolemy II Philadelphus, as coregent; reintroduced the tradition of brothers and sisters marrying to strengthen the family line; built many temples; and introduced a new god, Serapis, who was a combination of Greek gods as well as the Egyptian god, Osiris. The Ptolemy dynasty greatly promoted Greek ingenuity, learning, and arts, and even established the Great Library and Museum in Alexandria.

While the Ptolemy dynasty was able to achieve much power and wealth, the local Egyptians enjoyed little of this and the Greek population replaced them as the upper class, which led to many uprisings. After nearly three centuries, the final dynasty of Egypt ended with Cleopatra VII, the final Queen of Egypt. While she originally shared her rule first with her father, Ptolemy XII, she later ruled with her brothers, the XIII, and the XIV, both of which she was married to. However, her bother and spouse, Ptolemy XIII, ousted her from this rulership. Cleopatra was able to regain her throne by later on appealing to the Roman dictator Gaius Julius Caesar. Both of her brothers and husbands ended up dying, Ptolemy XIII drowned while attempting to cross the Nile, and while it cannot be proved, many people believe that Cleopatra poisoned Ptolemy XIV.

With the death of Cleopatra VII's brothers, she instated her son, Caesarion, who was fathered by Caesar, as her co-regent. The two of them appear together in a scene at the Temple of Hathor in Denderah.

Cleopatra entered a relationship with Mark Anthony of Rome. While he had most likely originally planned on turning Egypt into a Roman city, Cleopatra VII was able to change his mind with her exceptional personal and political skills. After the two spent much time together in Alexandria, they incurred the wrath of the Roman Senate and Augustus, who was Mark Anthony's brother-in-law. Rome most likely viewed the alliance between Cleopatra and Mark Anthony as a threat to the Roman rule. Augustus convinced everyone that Mark Anthony was a traitor and he declared war on the couple. After Cleopatra's and Mark Anthony's defeat in Greece in the Battle of Actium in 51 BC, the two fled back to Alexandria, where they stayed for ten months. Rather than undergoing the humiliation and imprisonment that the Roman Empire would impose on them, the two chose to commit suicide instead.

Roman Egypt: 30 BC – c.600 AD

Egypt became a part of the Roman Empire and lost independence, and Augustus Gaius Julius Octavianus was declared Pharaoh of all of Egypt on August 31st, 30 BC. Yet, unlike the other provinces under the Roman rule which were governed by the Senate, Augustus claimed Egypt as his personal property and appointed a vice-regal governor to report directly to him.

Egypt no longer had its own king, capital or law. While the stability and strength of the Roman Empire ensured that Egypt was profitable and governed successfully, Rome used this for their own good and the native Egyptians received none of the benefits of this wealth.

Chapter 2: The Egyptian Gods and Religion

Not much is known about religion during the Predynastic Period of Egypt. Yet, it is known that they worshipped a variety of animals such as jackals, dogs, sheep, and cows. These animals would sometimes be wrapped in linen and buried next to the Egyptians. These animals were also depicted in pendants, statues, pallets, and pottery. The form these animal deities took could also vary widely. Sometimes, these animal gods would be in full animal form, sometimes, full human form or sometimes, something in-between with characteristics that are both human and animal. One example of this is the god Khepri who would appear as either a scarab beetle or a man's body with the head of a scarab.

During the Predynastic Period when the various nations, which would later be unified into Egypt, would declare war with one another, the victor would often take on aspects of the loser's gods. They would do this by taking the desirable attributes and adding it to the legend of their own god, adding them to their god as a follower or the god would be forgotten altogether.

By the time of the Old Kingdom, there were so many gods that it caused much confusion, which led to the mistaken belief that the Egyptians had worshiped many gods. In truth, most Egyptians most likely only worshiped one god or a group of local gods. In order to make sense of the chaos, the priesthood would group the gods into families or into groups of either eight or nine depending on the area and temples. Various creation myths were also created for these different groups. Some of these gods, such as Ra, Amun, Osiris, and Isis continued to have the most power associated with them and more followers throughout the various time periods of ancient Egypt, sometimes, even gaining international worship.

The Heliopolitan Ennead

The group of nine gods was the most commonly held creation myth and religious belief in Ancient Egypt. The myth was that Amun, meaning the Complete One, was created out of the ocean, either as the son of the Ocean (Nun) or by self-creation so that he could, in turn, create the world. Amun was then said to bring forth land to stand on, which was supposedly where the temple of Heliopolis was later built. He was later associated with the sun god, Ra, so that he became known as Amun-Ra and was specifically believed to be tied to the evening sun. When Amun became Amun-Ra, he was seen as both visible and invisible, which appealed to the ancient Egyptians' desire for balance. Amun was depicted in art as a snake, goose, or ram, but also as a man with the head of a crocodile, royal cobra, frog, ape or a ram.

Since Amun was alone in the world, he then created a son and a daughter. His son Shu, the god of air, was brought forth by spitting him out of Amun's own substance. His daughter Tefnut, the goddess of water, was created when he vomited her out.

His children Shu and Tefnut then married and continued the process of creation by giving birth to a son and a daughter as well. Their son, Geb, was the god of earth and their daughter, Nut, was the goddess of the heavens. These gods, therefore, completed all of the cosmic gods needed for creation: sun, air, water, earth, and heaven.

The union of Nut and Geb resulted in the birth of the gods Osiris and Set as well as the goddesses Nephthys and Isis.

While these last gods and goddesses were not cosmic gods in nature, they were still some of the most important gods in Egyptian mythology.

Amun-Ra was said to be the father and protector of the Pharaoh, and the queens or princesses would sometimes be bestowed the title of Wife of Amun. The female Pharaoh, Hatshepsut, claimed that the throne was hers by right, saying her mother had been impregnated by Amun making her the natural heir.

While Amun's worship was overthrown during the reign of Pharaoh Akhenaten, when he replaced it with the worship of Aten, this only lasted during his reign and was reversed during the reign of his son, Tutankhamun.

Anubis

Not only was respect of the dead important to the ancient Egyptians, but preservation and preparation for the afterlife were also equally as important. To this end, the ancient Egyptians develop an extensive mummification process, would build pyramids, and bury the dead with artifacts to help them in the afterlife. The god Anubis was the deity of embalming and cemeteries, and would, therefore, protect the graves. Anubis was also said to guard the Hall of the Two Truths so that he could measure the hearts of people in judgment.

Anubis was depicted with the head of the black jackal. The reason for this was because jackals were known to wander around grave sites and would eat decomposing bodies. Egyptians hoped that if Anubis was the patron god of jackals, then it might prevent the bodies of their loved ones from being eaten. He was depicted in the color black as this was a symbol of good luck. The fertile soil of the Nile that allowed the Egyptians to grow their yearly supplies of food was dark black, therefore this color symbolized rebirth and good fortune.

Bastet

Bastet, the goddess of health, protection, and pleasure had the body of a slender woman and the head of a cat. She was said to be the daughter of Ra and sister of Sekhmet, as well as being the wife of Ptah and the mother to Mihos. It was believed that Bastet would ride through the sky with Ra to protect him, and then in the evening, she would transform into a cat and protect Ra from the serpent, Apep, who was his greatest enemy.

Cats were worshiped alongside Bastet, as they were considered the physical form of the goddess and were believed to be demigods. The cats could also aid the Egyptians by killing rats which slowed the spread of disease and by protecting their crops.

Ra

The Egyptians believed that they were blessed with the sun from Ra. Due to living in the desert and greatly relying upon the crops that the Nile and sun-blessed them with, the Egyptians were thankful for the sun and what it provided them with. They believed Ra was their patron deity of the sun, light, heaven, and power. Not only did he control the sun, but they believed that the sun was a physical manifestation of Ra himself.

Ra was often combined with other gods, as well. For instance, when he was commonly combined with Amun, he was known as Amun-Ra, which represented the original creation and the raw power of the sun. Ra might sometimes appear as his loving daughter, Hathor, or as his fierce and protective daughter, Sekhmet.

He could also be combined with Horus to become Ra-Horakhty, which means "Ra-Horus in the horizon". In this form, Horus would represent Ra incarnate as the reigning Pharaoh. Ra was also said to become Khepri to move the sun across the horizon before bearing it upon a mythical barge back through the underworld.

Isis

Another of the most beloved Egyptian gods was Aset, though she is now better known by her Greek name, Isis. Her name literally means "Queen of the Throne", and this is shown in her attire, especially her headdress which is frequently depicted as a throne. However, Isis could also be displayed with a disk and horns in honor of Hathor or the headdress of a vulture, which is associated with the goddess Mut.

Isis, also known as the great mother, was the wife and sister of Osiris, who ruled the underworld. In fact, the tale of Isis and Osiris was commonly believed to be a true love story. It was often said that the two were so in love with one another that they fell in love while they were still in the womb.

While Isis was originally appreciated only after her husband, Osiris, her believers, later on, transformed her into the Queen of the Universe. The Egyptians came to believe that Isis was the very embodiment of the cosmic order, and by the time Egypt fell, they held that she could control the very strings of fate. Some of the powers she was especially known for controlling were healing, the protection of women, and magic.

Sekhmet

The daughter of Ra and goddess of the hot desert sun as well as healing, chaos, and war, Sekhmet was a powerful goddess whose very name meant "she who is powerful and "the one who loves Ma'at" (Ma'at being a goddess of balance, truth, and justice). She was said to have been created by Ra in order to punish and destroy the humans who would disobey him and go against the order of Ma'at.

Sekhmet would transform into the goddess, Bastet, in cat form when she was calm, and when she was battling in a war, she would fiercely protect the Pharaohs and lead them in battle. She could be terrifying when she was protecting or punishing people, but she was also fiercely loved for curing the disease and averting the plague. She was the patron deity of healers and physicians, and the people would offer her prayers, food, drink, incense, and music in hopes Sekhmet would answer their prayers. This goddess was most often illustrated with the body of a woman and the head of a lion being illuminated by the disk of the sun.

These are only some of the gods of the ancient Egyptian belief system. There were many more, some of which were Bes, Hathor, Horus, Neith, Nephthys, Ptah, Sobek, and Thoth.

Chapter 3: The Kings of Egypt

There were a great number of powerful and impactful Pharaohs in Egyptian history. While covering every Pharaoh would take an entire book, this chapter will explore some of the kings of ancient Egypt that not only impacted their own country but also the world at large.

Menes – Archaic Period

While being the first Pharaoh of ancient Egypt means that there is not as much known about Menes as the later Pharaohs, he had a lasting impact on all of Egypt. Menes successfully unified Egypt and turned it into one kingdom, which would soon become an empire. He also built the first capital known as White Walls, which would later become known as the infamous Memphis.

Djoser – The Old Kingdom

The king during the third dynasty and most likely the first Pharaoh of the Old Kingdom, Djoser's reputation survived for centuries as a great leader and the first Pharaoh to introduce the custom of burying royalty in pyramids. Djoser's architect who designed his tomb was Imhotep, and this pyramid is known as the Step Pyramid in Saqqara.

Cheops – The Old Kingdom

Khufu, known as Cheops from the Greek language, was one of the Pharaohs in the fourth dynasty. While the Greek historian, Herodotus, represented Cheops as a tyrant, this king was also known to be knowledgeable with great wisdom. Cheops held great power and ruled over all of Egypt unchallenged. This allowed him to have the Great Pyramid of Giza built and write the Hermetic books.

Chephren – The Old Kingdom

Another king of the fourth dynasty, Chephren, originally known as Khafre, was the son of Cheops. This Pharaoh also had a pyramid built for himself in Giza, and this pyramid is the best-preserved example we have of these ancient monuments. Part of this pyramid's design includes the Great Sphinx, which supposedly incorporates some of Chephren's own facial features. According to Herodotus, Chephren was despised by his people as a cruel tyrant.

Mycerinus – The Old Kingdom

The last great king of the fourth dynasty, Mycerinus continued to build pyramids and sculptures. Unlike his father, Chephren, Mycerinus was described as being an extremely kind and just ruler over his people.

Mentuhotep Nebhepetre – First Intermediate Period

After the long period of conflict and civil war, Mentuhotep Nebhepetre was able to reunite ancient Egypt and become the first leader of the eleventh dynasty. In order to become Pharaoh, Mentuhotep subdued the Heracleopolis princes and regained control of Nubia. He also made Thebes his capital, built extensively there, and established Montu, a god of war, as the patron deity of this line.

Amenemhet I – Middle Kingdom

Amenemhet I was not born of royalty, but was rather the vizier of the previous Pharaoh, before usurping the throne and claiming it for himself. This led Amenemhet I to becoming the first ruler of the twelfth dynasty. During his rule, Amenemhet I campaigned in Nubia, traded extensively with Palestine and Syria, set It-towy as his capital city, created a system of coregency to protect his line of succession, and established the further worship of Amun in Thebes.

Amosis I – New Kingdom

The founder of the eighteenth dynasty, Amosis I, was the son of Seqenenre Ta'o and Ahhotpe, and his niece was Ahmose-Nefertari, who would become his chief queen. He became the first Pharaoh of his dynasty after pursuing the Hyksos out of Egypt. He set his capital city as Thebes, where he promoted the worship of Amun-Ra. Amosis I was able to successfully reestablish the Egyptian government to create a time of peace for his people and successors.

Tuthmosis I – the New Kingdom

While Tuthmosis I was the son of the previous Pharaoh, Amenhotep I, his mother was not royal. Therefore, in order to take the throne, Tuthmosis married his aunt, Princess Ahmose. Tuthmosis was a great military leader who campaigned far into Nubia territory, where he established multiple fortresses. He was also able to extend Egypt's power further into Syria. Tuthmosis was the first Pharaoh to be buried in the Valley of Kings in Thebes.

Tuthmosis III – New Kingdom

Tuthmosis was believed to be Egypt's greatest Pharaoh, yet at the beginning of his reign in the eighteenth dynasty, he was unable to rule. Since Tuthmosis was still a child when he ascended the throne, his stepmother Hatshepsut prevented him from the ruling. When he got older, he seized the true power of the throne from her and then attempted to erase all signs of her rule.

Tuthmosis III was a great military leader who conquered much of Palatine, Syria, and the Mitannians. He also began building many great temples, monuments, and other architecture.

Akhenaten (Amenhotep IV) – New Kingdom

Another Pharaoh from the eighteenth dynasty, Akhenaten was the son of Amenhotep III and Tiye. While his original name was Amenhotep IV, he changed it to Akhenaten during his fifth year on the throne, in honor of his preferred god, Aten.

Akhenaten and his wife, Nefertiti, greatly changed the religious aspects of Egypt at the time. They promoted monotheism and wanted sole worship to Aten or the sun disk. He disbanded the priesthood of other gods while strengthening that of Aten, he changed the capital city from Thebes to Tell el-Amarna and encouraged the arts there to focus on Aten.

While Akhenaten and Nefertiti had six daughters, they had no male heirs. Therefore, Akhenaten's brother became his coregent.

Akhenaten was regularly at war with the priesthood and temples of the other gods and was seen as a fanatic and opportunist. After his reign, the religious climate of Egypt reverted back to that of before his reign.

Ramesses II – New Kingdom

The son of Sethos I, Ramesses the II was a Pharaoh of the nineteenth dynasty that was famous for his prowess in war. While originally battling against the Hittites, Ramesses was able to eventually broker peace between the two nations during his twenty-first year on the throne. In order to formalize this peace, he married a Hittite princess, though he had many other wives and fathered more than one-hundred children. Ramesses had many great pieces of architecture built including monuments in Thebes, Memphis, Pi-Ramesse, Abu Simbel, and Abydos.

Ramesses II is hypothesized to possibly be the Pharaoh involved in the Biblical Exodus.

Ramesses III – New Kingdom

Son of Setnakhte and Queen Tiye-Merenese, Ramesses III was a Pharaoh of the twentieth dynasty and known as the last of the great warrior kings. Ramesses III successfully defeated the Libyans and the Sea People when they attempted to conquer Egypt. These famous battles were recorded in the Great Papyrus Harris, and also at the temple in Medinet Habu.

Ramesses successfully avoided an assassination attack from the women in the royal harem. Though, his reign was troubled by frequent strikes from the workmen of the royal necropolis.

Ptolemy I Soter – Ptolemaic Period

The first king of the Ptolemaic dynasty, he was left in charge as a satrap by Alexander the Great, and then took over the throne once Alexander died of illness. When Ptolemy I became the Pharaoh, he reorganized the government, reinstituted the local temples, introduced the worship of the new god Serapis. Ptolemy I Soter even created the infamous library and museum in Alexandria.

Ptolemy also brought back the tradition of marriages to close family relatives such as siblings. In this way, he was able to protect his line and dynasty.

Chapter 4: The Queens of Egypt

While many people may look down on princesses and queens as being a childish fantasy that little girls want to be and should grow out, the royal women throughout history were not only powerful, but they would make great sacrifices to benefit their people. There were many amazing Egyptian queens, whether they ruled from the throne or stood beside the Pharaoh supporting him in his role.

In times of peace, the Egyptian queens were expected to support the Pharaoh and the kingdom behind the scenes, along with their role of producing heirs to the throne. However, in times of turmoil and war, the Egyptian queen was expected to be intelligent and battle worthy, able to reign from the throne, protect the kingdom, and avoid assassination attempts.

While the Pharaoh may have many wives, the wife with the title of the queen was the wife who had an official role in both religious and political matters. She was the queen consort. These queens were separated from the other wives in their duties and titles, and would often be referred to as the "King's Great Wife". If the queen was able to produce an heir, she would later be known as the "King's Mother". If something happened to the queen's husband and the heir was still a child, the queen would most likely rule in the heir's place until he came of age.

The queen consort was likely not chosen lightly due to the importance of this role, and either the heir and husband-to-be would choose who to marry for this role or the reigning Pharaoh would choose for his heir. In order to keep the bloodline as close as possible, the ideal wife was someone of the royal family, often a sister or a half-sister who would grow up knowing what role they would someday likely have and preparing for it. However, there were some commoner queens such as Tiye and Nefertiti.

In some rare cases, there were even daughter-father marriages. Yet, only one of these marriages resulted in the birth of a child, which was a daughter, born from Ramesses II and his daughter Bintanath. Therefore, some people speculate that most of these marriages might not have been true marriages. Instead, most of these marriages might have merely been bestowed as a title to afford an unwed princess more power, perhaps so that she could act as a deputy and assist the queen consort.

Along with the King's Great Wife, the king also had remarkable palaces built solely as harems, where many of his wives, sisters, aunts, and their children would live. Not only did this arrangement provide the Pharaoh an opportunity to flaunt his wealth, but it ensured that if the Great Wife was unable to produce an heir or the heir died, there would be an ample number of princes who were already trained for the position. Though, this arrangement could also pose difficulties if there were too many princes of equal status, as this could confuse the line of succession. Some of the wives may also become ambitious, which could pose risk to the throne. While all of the Pharaoh's wives were queens, they were by no means equal; many of them possess no real power.

Khentkawes I

The Queen of the fifth dynasty, Khentkawes I was discovered in a tomb that was built on a natural outcrop of rock, giving it the appearance of being a combination of both a mastaba and a royal pyramid. This tomb included an antechamber, mortuary temple, storerooms, burial chamber, and even a section to house priests who would serve her cult.

Inscriptions of Khentkawes I's titles were found in her tomb, which has left Egyptologists debating on the meaning. The inscription was originally translated as "Mother of Two Kings of Upper and Lower Egypt", meaning she was the mother of the kings, Sahure and Neferirkare from the fifth dynasty. Although it is now believed that the more accurate translation is most likely "King of Upper and Lower Egypt and Mother of the King of Upper and Lower Egypt". The reason for this is because there is a display of Khentkawes in the tomb showing her sitting on a throne while she holds a scepter and wears a false beard and uraeus. The uraeus traditionally indicated kingship and tied the wearer to the snake goddess, Wadjyt. While later on queens would be depicted wearing the uraeus, at this point in time, it was reserved for the ruler. Therefore, it is believed that Khentkawes was a temporary ruler of Egypt, most likely in the role of a regent while her sons were young.

Ahmose-Nefertari

Pharaoh Ahmose married his sisters, Ahmose-Nefertari and Ahmose-Nebta. His sister and wife, Ahmose-Nefertari became his queen consort and had the titles of King's Daughter, King's Sister, and King's Great Wife, as well as the title God's Wife of Amun. This last title gave her great wealth, power, lands, and male attendants. She also held another and unrelated religious position, that of Divine Adoratrice, which brought her even more wealth and power. Ahmose-Nefertari used this wealth and power to make significant donations throughout Egypt, which resulted in her name being recorded in many temples.

It is suggested that she was also powerful politically. Her name has been found recorded beside the Pharaoh's on a number of occasions. In one occasion, it was written that he first discussed his plans regarding building the Abydos cenotaph with a "companion", suspected to be Ahmose-Nefertari. Ahmose-Nefertari gave birth to at least five daughters and four sons, five of which died during childhood. After the death of Ahmose, she acted as regent for her child, and when her son's childless wife passed away, she continued her role as consort to aid him.

Hatshepsut

Pharaoh Thutmose II married his half-sister, Hatshepsut. While she had the titles King's Daughter, King's Sister, and King's Great Wife, her preferred title was the inhered religious title, God's Wife of Amun. During this time, she began to build a consort tomb, although, it was abandoned before the building of the burial chamber was complete.

As the King's Great Wife, Hatshepsut began her role as queen consort. But, once her husband died, she took on the role of regent. Not for her own son, as she only had a daughter, but rather for the son of one of the Pharaoh's other wives, Isis. This wife was not considered to be of sufficient status to have the role of regent. Therefore, Hatshepsut took over this role with her stepson, Thutmose III. However, Thutmose III greatly loved his mother that he posthumously promoted her titles to King's Great Wife and God's Wife.

While Hatshepsut originally acted like a typical regent, she gradually gave herself more power. She was not afraid to overturn tradition, and by the seventh year of being a regent, she was crowned as king. While she was careful not to forget Thutmose III and always had him acknowledged as co-ruler, there was no mistaking the fact that Hatshepsut was the dominant and more powerful king. Thutmose III would not gain anywhere near the power that Hatshepsut held until the near the end of her life, which was in her seventies.

Once Hatshepsut became king, she took on a more masculine role, most likely to secure her reign. She went so far as to make the statues and monuments depicting her use a male figure, rather than the female figure she had been displayed with when she was queen consort. In order to secure her reign further, she also claimed that Amun was her father. Whether she actually believed this is unknown, but she had images of Amun falling in love with her mother, before transforming himself to look like the Pharaoh, and then Amun and her mother, Queen Ahmose, conceiving Hatshepsut. The story then goes into telling how the gods helped deliver Hatshepsut during her birth.

There seems to have been no opposition to Hatshepsut's rise to power, though even if there was, it is unlikely that the Egyptians would leave many records of it. It is likely that the reason for her rise to power was due to a political crisis which required an adult king. After becoming king, Hatshepsut began to replace her late husband's advisers with those from humble beginnings. This meant that the advisers had a vested interest in keeping Hatshepsut in power so that they themselves could retain power.

As Hatshepsut was required to keep her masculine portrayal in order to stay king, she also had to remain single. Yet, it is believed that she and a Steward of Amun, Senenmut, were lovers. While some crudely carved graffiti depicts Hatshepsut and Senenmut standing while having sex, there is more ample evidence that indicates they were likely lovers. In fact, Senenmut carved his own image into Hatshepsut's mortuary temple, which would be both daring and unprecedented for someone who wasn't a royal. Senenmut went so far as to build his tomb near Deir el-Bahari, which is where Hatshepsut had a temple built. Doing these things without the direct approval of the Pharaoh would have been disastrous.

Tiye

By his second year reigning as Pharaoh, Amenhotep III married Tiye as his queen consort. There were a couple odd things about this arrangement. Firstly, she was not of royal blood, as was standard. Though Tiye's family was high class and her father possessed a number of titles, it is possible that they may have even been linked to Queen Mutemwia in some way. Secondly, while the royal weddings were typically private affairs with no known dates, Amenhotep III sent out announcements across the kingdom announcing Tiye as his wife and queen consort.

Tiye was likely only an early teenager when she was first married, yet she and Amenhotep experienced a long and peaceful reign. This time of peace greatly affected the arts, and many sculptures were made of the two. Though, there would be more artistic depictions of the two if the following Pharaoh, Ramesses II, hadn't altered the artwork of Amenhotep and Tiye into a depiction of himself and his wife, Nefertari.

Tiye was an incredibly powerful queen and much more promenade than was the norm. She even played a big role in diplomatic affairs outside of Egypt. The time of Tiye's death is not known, though there is evidence to show that she died after her husband, and at least nine years into the reign of her son, Amenhotep IV.

Nefertiti

Like her mother-in-law before her, Nefertiti was not a member of the Egyptian royal family and very little is known about her family. Nothing is known of her parents, though she did have a sister by the name of Mutnodjmet. Some of the speculations of Nefertiti's origins are that she was a foreigner, possibly the Mittani princess Tadukhipa under a new name or a member of the Egyptian elite. One of the common theories is that Ay was her father, who was a grand vizier and would later become Pharaoh when Tutankhamun died without an heir. This is partly believed due to Nefertiti and Amenhotep IV being shown to give Ay and his wife Tiye necklaces of gold in their tomb, and the gift of gold from royalty was seen as a great honor upon a man, and unheard of for a woman.

When Nefertiti and Amenhotep IV promoted the sole worship of Aten, there were many ceremonies that took both a man and a woman. While Amenhotep and Nefertiti would usually do these ceremonies together, when Amenhotep was not around, then Nefertiti would play the role of the king with their daughter acting out the feminine role.

There is much art depicting the royal couple, and in this, it is plain to see that unlike in most cases, Nefertiti held great power. In most depictions of Amenhotep and Nefertiti, she is displayed as an equal. While it has not been proven, it is possible that she was even a coregent with Amenhotep IV. What is less likely, but still possible, is that she may have even ruled Egypt as sole king after the death of Amenhotep.

Cleopatra VII

Cleopatra and her husband and brother, Ptolemy XIII came to rule Egypt with the enthusiasm of their people and with the blessing of the Roman government, who still had troops stationed in Egypt. The kingdom was deep in debt at the time that Cleopatra and her husband-brother took over and greatly declined. Despite the fact that the male coregent would usually be the more dominant one in the relationship, Cleopatra took over more power than her husband-brother, most likely due to being seven years older than him.

Cleopatra decided to give military aid to the Roman general, Pompey, which angered the Egyptians and is most likely the leading force as to why Ptolemy attempted to have her killed. Yet, Cleopatra successful escaped and raised an army to help take back her throne.

In order to gain the sole power of the throne, Ptolemy had Pompey killed and his head pickled. As Pompey was a rival to Julius Caesar, he had hoped to win Caesar's favor so that he could get rid of Cleopatra. When Caesar visited Alexandria, Ptolemy gifted the head of Pompey to Caesar. However, Cleopatra had already appealed to Caesar and he appointed her sole queen.

While in Alexandria, both Cleopatra and Caesar were trapped when the Egyptian people proclaimed the youngest princess, Arsinoe IV, as queen. While they waited a long winter barricaded in the palace awaiting Roman reinforcements, the two became allies and lovers. When the reinforcements came, Ptolemy fled and ended up drowning in the Nile while the short-lived queen of Egypt was captured and taken to Rome.

The now widowed Cleopatra had the full support of Rome and married her eleven-year-old brother, Ptolemy XIV, though she was already pregnant with a child by Caesar. She named him Ptolemy Caesar or Caesarion, but Caesar was already married and unable to publicly accept Caesarion as his son. However, shortly before he was assassinated, Caesar attempted to pass a law that would allow him to have two wives and a legitimate child that lived in a foreign land.

Before Caesar was assassinated, Cleopatra and her husband spend over a year in Rome on Cesar's private estates, though they returned once Caesar had died. Soon, thereafter, Ptolemy XIV quickly fell ill and died, and it is unknown whether it was by natural causes or assassination, possibly by Cleopatra herself. If Ptolemy's death was not by natural causes, it would have been logical for the death to be caused by Cleopatra, as this left her son the sole heir to the throne.

After the assassins of Caesar and Cleopatra's sister who had been in Rome, Rome was split in two. Caesar's legal heir, Octavian, ruled the western empire while Mark Antony ruled the eastern empire.

As the relationship between Cleopatra and Caesar had afforded her more power and protection, Cleopatra sought to replicate this by seducing another roman leader. However, she chose the wrong leader. Rather than seducing Octavian, she seduced the less experienced and less intelligent Mark Antony. She was successful and he fell for her, resulting in the birth of the twins Alexander Helios and Cleopatra Selene.

While Mark Antony and Cleopatra attempted to regain some of Egypt's former power, they were utterly unsuccessful. Rather, Octavian and his sister Octavia grew more powerful and displeased with Cleopatra and Mark Antony. This came to an end when Mark Antony would sit on a throne in Alexandria while parading his two sons and declaring them as kings of both Egypt and Rome. Octavian began a war against the couple, which caused both Antony and Cleopatra to flee. Cleopatra returned first to Alexandria a few weeks before

Antony. The two became trapped in the city and Cleopatra offered to abdicate the throne to her children but was ignored. Antony went off to fight his final battle, and as he did, Cleopatra barricaded herself in the mausoleum.

Mark Antony then received a false report that Cleopatra had committed suicide; therefore, he fell on his own sword, committing suicide himself. The dying Antony was taken back to Alexandria and pulled up the walls of the mausoleum where Cleopatra was barricaded so that he would die in her arms. Later, Cleopatra, the last queen of Egypt committed suicide on August 12th, 30 BC. It is not known how she died, as her body has never been found, but it is said that she had small pricks on her arm and most likely had brought an asp with her to commit suicide rather than surrender to Rome.

Chapter 5: The Great Pyramids, Temples, and Afterlife

The pyramids were important to the ancient Egyptians, and not only in order to honor the dead. This is because it was an Egyptian belief that the Pharaoh was a living embodiment of the falcon god, Horus. They believed that once a Pharaoh passed on, the incarnation of Horus moved onto the next Pharaoh, and the deceased Pharaoh was then associated with Osiris, the father of Horus. For this reason, it was also important to preserve the bodies into mummies.

These pyramids became a boost for the economy, as new towns would be developed in the area and livestock and produce would be raised, as well. While it was originally believed that the builders of the pyramids were slaves due to the Greek historian Herodotus, this has since been shown to be false. While the life of pyramids workers was not easy, the joints on the skeletons show signs of injury and arthritis, there is no evidence that they were slaves. Rather, the pyramids were built by the workers who moved to the towns and farms that were developed near the pyramids. These people were skilled craftsmen who were paid for their work. There has even been graffiti found that was left by these builders of the pyramids, in which they gave their group names such as "Friends of Khufu" or "Drunkards of Menkaure".

While the Egyptians believed the Pharaoh was Horus reincarnated, it did not stop them from seeking fair wages. In fact, when Ramesses III did not pay the craftsmen who were building the royal necropolis located in Del el-Medina on time, the workers organized a strike. In fact, this strike was one of the first recorded in history. While it was risky to organize a strike, the workers sat in the nearby temples and refused to leave until they received their due pay. These measures worked, and eventually, the workers received their hard-earned rations.

During the Old Kingdom, the truly large pyramids were formed, especially during the generations of Sneferu, Khufu, and Khafre, or rather the fourth to sixth dynasties. These were so large that if Sneferu did have the Meidum pyramid built, as Egyptologists commonly believe, then the stone for that pyramid combined with the stone for this other two pyramids contained more than 3.5-million cubic meters or 124-million cubic feet.

While these large pyramids were popular during the fourth dynasty, and the pyramids were still popular during the fifth and sixth dynasties, they reduced in size. During these dynasties, they pyramids were not only built on a much smaller scale but with small stones as well. While these medium-sized pyramids contained stone rubble fill which reduced the quality of the overall product, the Egyptians were able to maintain the same form and casing, but at a much lesser expense. Simultaneously, while the size of the tomb pyramids was being decreased, the size of the temple pyramids was being increased.

The building of pyramids was greatly reduced during the First Intermediate Period while chaos reigned. They made resurgence during times of peace such as during the Middle Kingdom. However, the size and build of the pyramid were no longer standardized during this time. During the Middle Kingdom, the pyramids were formed in a variety of sizes, the entrance was no longer consistently on the north side of the pyramids, and they could be built with either a core of small broken stones in casemate or a mud brick core. During the New Kingdom, the pyramids were built in a shared burial ground for the Pharaohs, such as the Valley of the Kings located near Thebes.

Traditionally, whether a tomb was for royalty or an elite member of society, it would contain at least two portions. Generally, located below ground was the burial chamber with a temple or chapel placed above. The temple was made to be an eternal dwelling place for the soul's ka (life force), and people could leave offerings and perform rituals there as well. The chamber of the temple was decorated in such a way that if the religious following fell away over time, the departed soul would still be provided with food and other items magically for an eternity.

When it was possible, these tombs, temples, and pyramids would be built along the western bank of the Nile River, where they could be linked to the setting of the sun.

There were many beliefs of the afterlife in ancient Egypt, just as there still are many views on whether or not there is one to this very day. One of the common beliefs was that after the funeral for a Pharaoh, he would join the sun god, Ra, on his daily journey across the sky. Then, during the night, the soul of the Pharaoh and Ra would travel through the underworld and fight off demons throughout the night so that they could then join with Osiris and become reborn at the sunrise. This daily journey was supposed to display the story of creation and create balance in the cosmos. Every morning at sunrise, the loved ones of the departed would then greet the sunrise, remembering the departed with gratitude for their efforts in the afterlife.

For this process to be a success, the Egyptians completed specific rituals. It was believed that at the time of death, a person's ba and ka separated from their bodies, or rather their life force and their soul. In order for the person to survive in the afterlife, their ka needed a supply of food, drink, clothing, and incense in their tomb for the afterlife. The ba was able to leave the tomb and temple, and visit and affect the lives of their loved ones or all of Egypt in the case of the Pharaoh. The body of the deceased was properly mummified by wrapping it in linen and removing aspects of the body that would rot, such as the brain. This was done so that the ba and the ka could live eternally with the mummified body as a vessel.

If something happened to the deceased's body, they were still able to attain the afterlife with statues or images of themselves in place of a body. Yet, it was necessary for their name to be forever remembered so that the gods could call them.

Chapter 6: The Nile and its Importance

Being a country largely made up of the desert, the ancient Egyptians greatly relied on the Nile and its yearly water levels. If the water levels were either too low or too high, it would spell death for many Egyptians, especially the impoverished. While much of the land is desert, the Delta, the Nile Valley, and the few oases found in the Western desert were all extremely fertile when the yearly water levels were balanced.

During the Paleolithic Period (c.5,000 BC) of what would later be ancient Egypt, much of these areas were uninhabitable, making life more harsh and difficult for the people. This is because every year, the Nile will flood, watering the surrounding areas and fertilizing them. However, this flood lasts for three months of the year and would destroy any residences in the area. During this time, people lived in the desert areas and hunted wildlife to survive.

Then, as the climate changed during the Neolithic period about 1,000 years later, people were slowly able to move closer to the Nile and this fertile ground. This allowed people to begin living in communities, grow agriculture, and develop a cultural belief system. Due to the environment having such a large impact on their daily lives and survival, this naturally developed into the belief that it was due to the sun god, Ra. Witnessing the yearly floods which fertilized and rejuvenated the land inspired their belief in Osiris.

During the Predynastic Period, these people continued to be drawn together. They built larger towns and cities for their mutual protection until they eventually organized themselves into two separate kingdoms known as the White Land and Red Land. Even after the Predynastic period, when the kingdoms were combined into one, Egypt never forgot its roots and the two lands remained distinctive.

While Egypt only receives a trivial amount of annual rainfall, due to the occurrence of the inundation (flooding) of the Nile, its people are able to flourish. This is especially true for those in the Delta and the Nile Valley where the temperatures are more moderate than in Upper Egypt where they receive the blessing of the water from the Nile.

This inundation was caused by high levels of rainfall in Ethiopia. This water would travel down the Nile until it overflowed in the Delta, creating marshlands for three months out of the year. This event usually began at the end of June or beginning of July and ended in late September. The exact timing would vary depending on how far into Egypt you were.

This event was seen as an annual miracle from the gods Osiris and Hapy. Although, there was always fear that the Nile might not rise one year. If the Nile did not rise, it would result in the death of thousands of ancient Egyptians and destruction. While the Nile always rose, there were times when it was low and greatly affected the population. If the Nile did not rise enough, it would bring forth devastation and famine. In fact, if the Nile flooded excessively, this would also cause famine, as the crops would be overly flooded causing the food to rot. Due to this, the ancient Egyptians studied the habits of the Nile River and closely measured both its rise and fall throughout the years. They developed a system of written records in order to track the Nile, which may have contributed to their development of hieroglyphic writing. The ancient Egyptians learned that in order to have a bountiful harvest and prevent disaster, the yearly inundation of the Nile River needed to rise above sixteen cubits as it entered the Delta, but rise no more than eighteen cubits.

In order to promote the inundation of the Nile, the ancient Egyptians performed rituals in which they would throw female fertility figures, sacred jewelry, fruit, cake, and sacrificial animals into the Nile. This was believed to promote its fertility, therefore, providing the Egyptians with the water their crops needed.

The ancient Egyptians learned early on that in order to have a successful harvest and survive, they needed to have some degree of control over the Nile and its yearly inundation. To this end, a predynastic ruler, known as Scorpion, began the process of building canals and dikes throughout the Nile Valley and Delta. This process gave the people of Egypt a common goal, which brought them together and aided in the unification of Egypt into one kingdom.

This irrigation system the ancient Egyptians built was very complex, which is no surprise when you look at the complex pyramids and temples that they also built.

This system used canals created on either side of the Nile River to convert water as far inland as possible. Earthen dikes were then used to divide the land into portions which the water would be converted to through the canals when the inundation occurred. The water would remain in this area until the Nile deposited its rich and fertile soil. The water would be drained off, and then the soil of the Nile would be worked into their crops as a fertilizer to promote the health and fertility of the plants.

Most of ancient Egypt's people worked on the land, cultivating the crops either for the needs of their family or the kingdom. This took much effort from the entire populace. Therefore, the government organized the irrigation of the Nile

River to the crops, and would then store the country's food supply in granaries, in case of famine.

The main crop in Egypt was grain, which had been introduced to the ancient Egyptians during the Neolithic time period from the near east. Illustrations of how these grains were grown were frequently carved into tombs, to provide the deceased with ample food during the afterlife. The grains that were mostly grown were types of wheat, known as spelt and emmer, which provided the Egyptians with their staple of bread and beer.

After the yearly inundation, during the late months of the year, the Egyptians would begin their period of growth. To achieve this, they would scatter the seeds across the field, which was then plowed by hand with a hoe or with the aid of cows with a plow attached. After the seeds were scattered and plowed, livestock was let loose into the field which caused the seeds to be easily pushed down into the soil, providing them with enough soil depth to grow. Whereas, the grains that made up a large portion of the Egyptians diet could only be grown once a year after the inundation.

The people were also talented gardeners. They would often grow these gardens near the cultivated canals or basins where the plants could easily be watered. When the gardens were further away from the canals and near their houses, they would carry water in large pots suspended by a yoke in order to water the plants. Some of the most often grown produce included lentils, chickpeas, beans, fenugreek, onions, radishes, lettuce, cucumbers, herbs, grapes, figs, sycamore figs, pomegranates, olives, and dates. Some of these plants would even be turned into oils, dyes, perfumes, and wine.

Chapter 7: The Daily Life of Ancient Egyptians

While much of our knowledge of the ancient Egyptian period comes from their tombs, pyramids, and temples, some amount of their daily life has been understood by this. The Egyptians craved creating a prosperous after-life and would leave inscriptions and art depicting this in their tombs. From this evidence, archaeologists have been able to understand what was important to the ancient Egyptians and glean an understanding of their daily lives.

The cities were built around the Nile River. In early periods, there would be small houses on both sides of the river, and people would have close contact with whichever neighbors were to their immediate north or south. As the Nile was their source of water and means of transport, these habitations around the river slowly grew until they would often become large cities. However, they left the fields in the most fertile areas around the river to grow their crops.

The population of ancient Egypt cannot be accurately determined. While it is believed that the population was rather dense, and the sizes of the cities support this, there are no hard figures to analyze. For instance, the military records may say "one hundred thousand persons," but it is likely that this is not a hard number, and instead, was meant to signify a large number of people rather than a specific number.

While there was a mixture of races in ancient Egypt, all of the exact races are unknown. Many people settled down in Egypt at different time periods. There were prisoners of war, foreign rulers, traders, craftsmen, technicians, and diplomats who traveled there from other countries. Despite this influx of foreigners, Egypt was able to remain largely stable in its beliefs and traditions, as they were left in solitude during their most formative years. Yet, the Greeks did have a large impact on Egyptian civilization.

While the ancient Egyptians did believe that men and women had different roles in marriage, in some aspects, they were much more forward-thinking than others at their time. In fact, the financial status of both women and children was protected under the law. If a woman was married, she would retain the rights to any property she owned, and if her husband divorced her, then she would retain her land and the ex-husband would be required to pay her compensation. The Egyptian's texts of wisdom instructed for husbands to care for their wives by feeding and clothing them, loving them, and seeking to please them.

It was advised for a man to marry as soon as he owned property and was of the age of twenty so that he could have children while he was young. Unlike in the royal family, it was no common to marry close relatives or have multiple spouses. Marriages were not a fancy affair in ancient Egypt. While gifts would be given at the betrothal, there is no record of celebrations, religious practices, or wedding traditions. The weddings were most likely a private legal ceremony.

After being married, a man was seen as the head of his household and the wife was seen as the mistress of the house. While they may have had different roles assigned to them by society, both had equal legal rights. The two owned the property together, and after death, the wife would have equal share to her husband's tomb and the afterlife.

While the Egyptians were devoted to their families due to the hardships of the land and the need to ration food, they most likely used contraceptives to limit the number of children they would bear. There is even a famous medical Papyrus which contains information on pregnancy, sterility, and contraceptives. Similar information can also be found in other Egyptian documents.

If a couple were unable to conceive, it was seen as a great tragedy. In this case, a female slave might bear the children of the father. These children would then have full legal rights of inheritance. The process of childbirth was a dangerous one, where the women frequently died in childbirth and children often did not live more than a few months.

Regarding slaves, they did not build the pyramids, but there were slaves owned by the elite and the royal families. While different from how many countries kept slaves, they were slaves all the same and their freedoms were restricted. Yet, these slaves did have the ability to own land, leave their property to their children as an inheritance, employ servants, and the men were able to marry a free woman.

The ancient Egyptians greatly loved animals, and it was not uncommon for them to own pets. These included the cat, dogs, monkeys, and ducks.

The Egyptians took great care of their personal appearance and hygiene. To remain clean, many women and men would shave their heads, and if they were in the middle or upper class, they would wear wigs when going outdoors. During the Old Kingdom, both sexes tended to keep short and simple hairstyles, but this changed in the New Kingdom. During this time, both women and men had long hair, which they would decorate with ribbons and flowers. Children's hair was also shaved off, but they would keep a lock of hair on the side of their head until they reached puberty. To promote hygiene, Egyptians would remove all body hair including facial hair.

Cosmetics were commonly used by both sexes, as well. These were originally developed to protect the skin from the hot desert sun, although they developed deodorants, perfumes, facial cleansers, anti-wrinkle creams, henna tattoos, eye paint, and Kohl eyeliner.

Conclusion

The ancient Egyptian life was not an easy one. The whims of the weather and the inundation of the Nile River could easily lead to either prosperity or ruin. Yet, its people came together and worked hard in order to survive. They created water channels and learned to plow fields, they made oils out of olives and argan, they grew herbs and fruits, and they stored grain in case they experienced famine.

The Egyptians would be invaded from time to time, by the Hyksos, Sea People, and others. They would experience economic decay, the ruination of dynasties, and the assassination of the Pharaohs. Yet, the people pulled together, fought off the invaders, and the Egyptian dynasty was able to last for thousands of years. They may have, at times, been subjugated to the rulership of foreign governments, but until the time the Roman Empire invaded, they were able to eventually dethrone the foreign kings and begin a new dynasty with their own people.

The kings and queens of Egypt were powerful. They were most often controlling all of both Lower and Upper Egypt while holding absolute power over politics, religion, and any other matter. There were tyrants, those known as heretics, and there were those who were just and loved by their people. While the male heir usually ruled the throne, in times of distress, a queen may take over, and she might even crown herself king.

There is still much to learn about ancient Egypt and the Egyptians' way of life, yet, archaeologists and Egyptologists are constantly making new discoveries, analyzing the evidence, and learning about this amazing first empire and its people.

Ancient Greece

A Concise Overview of the Greek History and Mythology Including Classical Greece, Hellenistic Greece, Roman Greece and The Byzantine Empire

Introduction

The following chapters will discuss the epic story of Ancient Greece throughout its varied and fascinating eras. We will begin our glorious journey of discovery in the very distant past that most of it is lost to the sands of time, and the stories that continue to live on do so mostly through myth and legend.

In chapter 1, we will travel back in time to Mycenaean Greece during the great Bronze Age. This epic period in civilization gave birth to bronze tools and weapons, and proto-writing. At its end, the Bronze Age saw a massive, global collapse that would claim the victory of most of the world's civilizations and plunge the entire world into the Dark Age. It is from the ashes of the Greek Dark Ages that Ancient Greece would rise.

In chapter 2, we begin our journey into the Greece of Classical Antiquity. Emerging first from this era was the Archaic period, which saw a dramatic increase in population and with it structural and social revolutions. More importantly, we will go through the crucial developments that transpired during this historic period.

On Classical Antiquity, chapter 3 elaborates on the vast history of Greece through its Classical Era. We will learn about the massive changes in Greek culture during this era that spanned a period of two centuries. This period marked a myriad of developments and progress in culture; the effects and principles of which we still see today.

Chapter 4 will then guide is through Ancient Greece's strong and proud Hellenistic period. This period saw the peak of Greek cultural influence and Alexander the Great conquest of nearly the entire known world. The Hellenistic period would then suffer decline and, ultimately, conquest by the Roman Empire – more in chapter 5 Interestingly, Greek culture continued to flourish during Roman reign.

Finally, in chapter 6, we will take a look at the events that transpired after the decline of Ancient Greece, most notably the rise and turbulent transition into the Byzantine Empire. We'll dig deep into the changing role that the old and noble civilization of Greece was to have down through history in its tumultuous path into the modern world.

There are plenty of books with this subject on the market, but we thank you for choosing this one! Every effort was made to ensure it is full of as much useful information as possible. Please enjoy!

Chapter 1: Mycenaean Greece and the Late Bronze Age Collapse

The entire epic and grand history of Ancient Greece was an ancient, long-lasting civilization that saw the birth of some of the most fundamental elements of our society today. These fundamental elements include many of the major core concepts of philosophy, the earliest and most enduring military tactics, and practices, as well as innovations in political thought that gave rise to democracy itself.

However, before we dive too deeply into the great coalition of ancient City-States known as Ancient Greece, it would be wise for us to take a brief look at the surrounding historical narrative that set the scene for its ascension. We'll a primer on much of the context and the pre-history of the region so we can get the deepest and firmest grasp on our topic as we possibly can.

The Ancient in Ancient Greece

A robust comprehension of the setting and historical context of Ancient Greece's eventual cultural innovations will mean going back to a basic understanding of Greek identity and how it was shaped by the preceding civilization. Also, we will look into the Dark Age that followed the culture's collapse. As a reference, we will be using the term "Classical Antiquity" to describe the period that was largely defined by the rise and decline of Ancient Greece. This period is in contrast to the previous period, which we broadly refer to as the Bronze Age.

The Bronze Age, of course, was not just a small blip in the great historical timeline. Rather, it was a grand period of human growth and cultural development. As it pertains to Greece, the

Bronze Age is generally referred to as the Helladic period by archaeologists of the modern era. This name is derived from the name Hellas, which was the name by which these early proto-Greek peoples called themselves. These modern archaeologists then subdivide the Helladic period into three distinct sub-periods. These sub-periods are known as the Early Helladic period, the Middle Helladic period, and finally, the Late Helladic period.

Mycenaean Greece

To understand the peoples of Ancient Greece, we will especially need to take a closer look at the era of the Late Helladic period and the culture that dominated the area during that time. This very early civilization was known as Mycenaean Greece, which was the prototypical society that would eventually form the basis for Ancient Greece many, many years later.

When we look at the Late Helladic period of Mycenaean Greek history, we can further divide this period into three even smaller sub-periods. These three sub-periods are commonly referred to as LHI, LHII, and LHIII. Again, we are going to take a particular interest on the latest of these periods, the LHIII, and examine how the highs and lows of this era shaped the Greek world to come. The LHIII is generally characterized as an era of great expansion that was followed by a sharp decline and finally a collapse that ended the Mycenaean civilization, along with many of their contemporary neighbors.

Many of this period's major innovations, which covered fields as broad as engineering, military infrastructure, and architecture, were first introduced by the Mycenaean Greeks. This period was also a time of vast and complex global trade that was crucial to the Mycenaean economy and societal infrastructure. In addition to all of these massive leaps in progress, Mycenaean Greece was home to one of the world's earlier forms of written script, which is known today to modern historians and linguists as the Linear B system. This very early system of written record gave us our first look at the Greek language. These records that have been miraculously preserved over the millennia also gave us our first records of Greek religion that at this point already included many of the figures and deities that would live on in the Olympic Pantheon in later generations of Greeks and Romans.

The societal structure of the Mycenaean culture at this time was a number of palace-based city-states dominated by a societal class of warrior elites and was held in place by rigid economic, social, and political systems.

Late Bronze Age Collapse

The very end of the Late Helladic era saw the Mycenaean culture perish in an event known to history as the Late Bronze Age collapse. The effects of this sudden and violent catastrophe were felt throughout the entire Eastern Mediterranean region, upon which all of the earliest and most advanced civilizations of the time were built. What followed was a period when the art of record keeping was lost and would not be seen again for several hundred years. This kind of cultural regression is what is known in retrospect as a Dark Age wherein an entire period is covered in a figurative darkness and records or historical writings that may shed light on the events that transpired do not exist.

The Late Bronze Age collapse affected not only the Mycenaeans but also many of the other dominant civilizations in the complex socio-economic structure of the Late Bronze Age world. Many of the most populous and prosperous cities in all of the Eastern Mediterranean, and by extension, the entire known world of the time, were either destroyed or abandoned. The exact reason for this collapse is unclear, but several theories have been put forward, including socio-economic unrest and upheaval, disruption to the complex network of trade routes, and popular uprisings. Perhaps the most intriguing, however, is the evidence of mysterious unknown invaders that contemporaries referred to as the 'Sea Peoples'.

It is unclear who exactly the Sea Peoples were, but several theories have been put forward. Some of these theories offer up relatively simple and mundane explanations, for example, some popular hypotheses suggest that the Sea Peoples may have been the Philistines, the Minoans, the inhabitants of the island of Crete, or any number of other island dwelling Mediterranean cultures. Perhaps even a grand coalition of a number of these societies and cultures. On the fringe side of things, many historians (often of questionable credentials) are firmly convinced that the Sea Peoples were invaders from the land of Atlantis. Atlantis of course being the almost certainly fictional society that Plato spoke of in one of his allegories. Realistically, though, the Sea Peoples could have been any number of Bronze Age societies in existence in and around the Mediterranean and the Fertile Crescent at the time.

In all likelihood, the collapse was probably a combination of all of these factors. In any case, the events of this period later became the basis for much of the literature and mythology of Ancient Greece, including the Trojan Epic. We may not know exactly who the Trojans were, or even if there was a literal city called Troy. And we can be fairly certain that the more fantastical and mythical elements of the tales are likely exaggeration or fabrications, we know that it was the tales from the Bronze Age, mythologized by generations of oral history, became much of the Greek and Roman mythology we know today.

In the Dark Age that followed this the Late Bronze Age Collapse, however, details are very scarce as to what was happening in the ancient world. The only one of the great civilizations to have survived the Late Bronze Age Collapse, although barely, and having suffered the loss of their written language and many other societal and technological advances, were the Egyptians, who interacted extensively with the Greeks at the time. But even the surviving records from the Egyptians, while confirming the invasions of the Sea Peoples and corroborating much of the evidence of social unrest and economic crisis during the era, they tell us very little about what the various peoples who survived the Dark Age did to survive, or what kind of lives they lived.

In any event, while the Late Bronze Age Collapse prevents us from having full knowledge of what our ancient ancestors did to survive a civilization-ending crisis, it does show us without any doubt that human beings certainly have the ability and the desire to survive. And the Mycenaeans, although devastated by profound and wide-ranging disaster did in fact survive. They survived, they adapted, they fought and eventually, they thrived. And these people, crawling out of the ashes of a doomed civilization, rose to become one of the greatest, most powerful and most culturally significant civilizations the world has ever seen.

This is the story of Ancient Greece.

Chapter 2: Archaic Greece

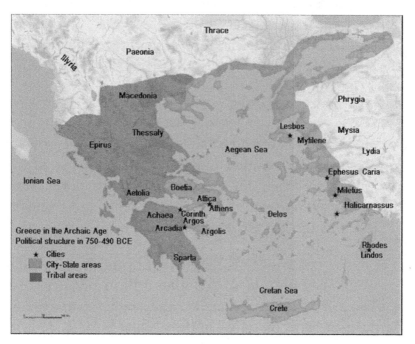

The world of the Ancient Mediterranean emerges from the period of Dark Ages firmly entrenched in what later became known as the Iron Age. For Greece, this brought about a period in its history that we today call Archaic Greece, and began immediately following the Greek Dark Ages in and around the eighth century BC. The beginning of this period was marked by sharp and large increases in the population of Greece. At the same time, a string of major social changes made the society Greece was becoming virtually unrecognizable to the Greece of the previous eras.

There were two major changes that became the basis for this period in Greek history. The first of these important changes was what has been termed the structural revolution which helped define the political map of the Ancient Greek world. This is the cultural revolution that brought to power the traditional Greek city-states such as Athens and Sparta. By the end of the Archaic period of Greek history, the second major revolution was taking place, the intellectual revolution. A reformation that would lead the major development of the Classical Period, which we will into in much greater detail in the next chapter.

The Archaic period of Ancient Greece saw a number of important development and broad growth in the areas of Greek culture, economics, politics, and international relations. The period was also when the Greeks started to develop their proclivity for warfare and developed the units and tactics that would lead them to military supremacy for centuries to come.

Also of major importance is the advent of the Greek alphabet which would lead to some of the other critical advances of this time. The earliest known Greek literature to have survived until modern times were composed in the Archaic period, along with many of the monuments and sculptures that directs our historians to this day.

The Archaic period of Greece is generally considered to have started at the time of the foundation of the Olympic Games. It took place in 776 BC and marks a major historical and cultural turning point. For a long time, the Greek Archaic period was considered to be of less historical importance than the later Classical and Hellenistic periods, but these attitudes have more recently changed. The Archaic periods is seen by experts with a renewed sense of importance.

One of the primary sources we have for information in this period is from the Greek writer Herodotus, usually called the first historian. While Herodotus often omits dates, and many of his writings could rightly be considered mythology.

Nevertheless, his accounts make up the basis of much of our knowledge.

Cultural Developments

The Archaic period of Ancient Greece was a time of major cultural development and social change. One of the biggest shifts of the period was the changes in the political landscape of the Greek world. Prior to this time, most settlements and cities were under the control of warlords and were essentially tribal bands with early, proto-democratic systems. In the Archaic period, Greece witnessed the development of the polis or city-state, as what we know today. During this time, the polis became the central point of political organization. While we tend to think of Ancient Greece as a type of nation or empire, this concept is not entirely correct. Ancient Greece should be more accurately thought of as a loose coalition of city-states that were culturally tied together by a common language.

Each of these city-states was self-organized and self-governed. Many of the individual city-states that made up Greece were ruled by leaders. Collectively, they are to be known as the tyrants. These tyrants governed with an early form of autocratic rule. At the same time, however, this period of Greek history also has come to show some of the earliest evidence for the development of constitutional structures and law codes, both of which indicate the birth of an early law system, as well of a form of community-based decision-making. By the end of the Archaic period of Ancient Greece, the two most dominant cities, Sparta and Athens, seem to have developed their respective constitutions. These constitutions' forms were maintained and would be considered their classical forms.

In eighth and seventh centuries BC, the people of the Greek cities began to spread out. Citizens settle throughout the Mediterranean, the Black Sea, and the Sea of Marmara. While much of this travel was done for the purpose of establishing and maintaining trade routes and contacts, these travels were also made in the interest of settling and securing new territory. These new settlements grew to become independent city-states of their own. The independent city-states are one of the primary distinguishing characteristics of Ancient Greece. It is important to note that the new settlements would be unlike the case under an empirical system, such as Rome or the British Empire of many centuries later.

There were two different and distinct ways in which the Ancient Greeks settled new territory outside of Greece. The first was the way in which a detachment of Greeks would found a city which would serve as an independent *polis*. The other form of Ancient Greek settlement in this period was what modern historians refer to as an emporium, or in the plural form *emporia*. These were essentially trading posts which were colonized and inhabited by Greeks and non-Greeks alike. The primary purpose of these emporia was to manufacture goods for sale and export.

Some of the first Greek colonies to have been founded at this time were located on the island known as Sicily. These early colonies were founded by people from various different city-states all around throughout Greece. By the waning years of the eighth century BC, there had also been a number of well-established Greek settlements throughout the southern regions of modern day Italy.

During the seventh century BC, the Greek colonists continued to expand throughout the areas in which they had settled and become established. In the more western reaches of the Greek culture, settlements were established as far away from the nucleus of Greek society as modern day Marseilles. On the eastern side of this cultural explosion, the Greek cultural spread reached well into the north of the Aegean, as well as throughout the Black Sea and the Sea of Marmara. Securing new territory and generating new colonists became a major part of the game of political dominance in this era of Greek history

Toward the end of the Archaic era, the Southern region of modern-day Italy and the entirety of what is Sicily today had received a massive influx of Greek colonizers. At this point, there had been so many Greek settlements founded within the reaches of southern Italy and Sicily that it had come to be called as Magna Graecia or Great Greece. Records indicate that land was being settled in the region at a rate of no less than one settlement for every other year. The pattern of rapid settlement continued throughout modern-day Italy well into the middle of the fifth century BC.

While this period was certainly a time of rapid growth and development, there was a darker side to the cultural spread. Today, the period of Archaic Greece is sometimes referred to as the Age of Tyrants. The Ancient Greek word *tyrannos*, from which we derive the modern word tyrant, was first seen in contemporary Greek literature of the time in a poem written by Archilochus. Tyrannos was used to describe Gyges, a Lydian ruler. The earliest Greek ruler who fits the description of a tyrant was the leader Cypselus, who took power by force in a coup during the year 655 BC. This was followed by a veritable trend of tyranny throughout the Archaic Greek word during the middle of the seventh century BC.

Many different explanations have been put forward to explain for the socio-political shift to tyranny as a ruling standard. One particularly notable example goes all the way back to the writings and teachings of Aristotle. He felt that tyranny was a natural side effect of the ruling class becomes more and more intolerable. He argued that tyrants were actually chosen and installed by the people as a reaction to a deeply unpopular ruling class. More modern approaches explain that the tyranny phenomenon has focused more on identifying powerful men that controlled large, private armies. They utilized intimidation to seize power. Other theories, suggests that it was oligarchs fighting among themselves that lead to tyranny, rather than the power struggles between these powerful oligarchs and the people.

It is important to note that the population of Greece doubled during the eighth century BC. The growth in population resulted in more settlements being founded further afield. These new settlements were even larger than they had been previously.

The population boom was not isolated to Greece. The upturn was actually part of a broader phenomenon of growth in population that was happening all across the Mediterranean area during this time. As we are more aware, large-scale population shifts and human activities of this nature can have a massive effect on the natural climate and environment. It is believed that the population growth that happened across the Mediterranean region during this period directly resulted in a notable climatic shift that occurred between the years of 850 BC and 750 BC. The climate of the region became much cooler and wetter than normal.

While this was certainly a period of rapid development and of intense land-seizure, there was still a fair amount of arable land that was not yet being used for cultivation in Greece in the Archaic period. Despite the fact that much land was available, and ever increasing as new settlements were founded, it seems that farms in this period were primarily concentrated very close to the established settlements. Farms were small, cohesive units.

Evidence shows that crop rotation practices had been well established by this point. It was particularly common to alternate between cereals and legumes. Farmers also allowed the land to be left fallow on alternating years to maintain ground nutrients.

The crops were also highly diversified and farmers tended to grow a large variety of crops simultaneously. This practice allowed for the more consistent use of human resources all throughout the year. The strategy also provided a degree of protection against crop failure, as it was highly unlikely for all of the various crops to fail during one season.

Apart from this manner of subsistence farming, the Ancient Greeks also cultivated a wide variety of luxury items and cash crops which they would sell both locally and abroad for great profit. Such cash crops included olives and vines, as well as various fruits and vegetable.

Livestock played an important role in the agriculture and economy but it was notably of secondary importance. Some domesticated animals, particularly goats and sheep, were kept for wool, milk, meat, and fertilizer. Livestock was very difficult to maintain. Average farmers may have kept a few animals for meat or milk, but large herds were prohibitively expensive to maintain. Owning a large herd is generally a sign of extreme wealth. For instance, a team of oxen would have gone a long way to significantly improve agricultural yields but it would be too expensive for the average farmer. Only the affluent would have been able to afford horses or particularly large herds of cattle.

Trade was absolutely fundamental to the economy and infrastructure of not only Greece but the entire Mediterranean region and the Aegean Sea by the later years of the eighth century BC. The advanced and extensive trade network led to a large degree of cultural exchange in the early days of Archaic Greece. An evidence is a strong oriental influence on Greek art.

As many of the Greek colonies throughout Southern Italy and Sicily became larger and more powerful, trade continued between them. The older, earlier Greek settlements throughout the Mediterranean. This led to a strengthening of cultural unity throughout the entire region and began to solidify Greece as a cultural and economic powerhouse.

The Greek islands as we know them today, where the central hub for eastern trade. It acted as an intermediary between mainland Greece and the lands of the east. Throughout this period and into the sixth century BC, the eastern Greek city-states became very, very prosperous on account of vast and robust trade routes with Egypt and Asia. Corinth, along with the other more coastal city-states of the Greek mainland, received the largest portions of the trade from the east.

Greek art from the various city-states also became a major element in trade during this period. It resulted in both the production and development of Greek art, along with serving to bolster Greek trade even further.

Visual arts during the Archaic period of Ancient Greece also underwent significant changes in style and craft. Many pieces of art have been preserved from this time. They can generally be characterized by more naturalistic and representational styles. Monumental sculpture was first introduced in the Greek world during this time. The art of pottery went through massive stylistic shifts. Both pottery and sculpture were both heavily influenced by oriental styles. The Archaic period of history in Ancient Greece also saw some major innovations in literature, notably including the advent and development of the Greek alphabet. We also have evidence that the earliest surviving Greek poetry was composed during this period.

When the Greek Dark Ages preceded the Ancient and Archaic periods of Greek history, the art and science of writing were lost in Greece. It is highly probable that by the ninth century BC, no one left in Greece would have been able to understand the Bronze Age Linear B system of writing. However, after the ninth century BC, there is evidence of objects being imported into the Greek that was inscribed with Phoenician writing. This Phoenician script formed the basis for what would eventually become the Greek Alphabet. Developed during the eighth century BC. By the middle years of the eighth century BC, pottery with Greek inscriptions begin to become evident.

These early inscriptions in the Greek alphabet generally tend to be for the purpose of identifying or explaining the object where it is inscribed.

Military Developments

During the Archaic period, the military experienced what many would consider one of the most historically important developments in the world. The development was the adoption of the Hoplite in warfare by the Greek city-states. This major adoption occurred during the earlier years of the seventh century BC. The Hoplite armor, called the panoply, appeared as early as the eighth century BC. The city-state of Argos was the location of the discovery of the earliest known examples of the panoply armor in the eighth century BC.

The panoply was composed of several different individual pieces of armor. Although individual pieces of arms and armor had been used and developed for centuries, the complete panoply cannot be proven to have been in use until about 675 BC. A Corinthian vase painting dated to this year has been found depicting a soldier equipped in the entire panoply.

In fact, the word panoply can be translated to something similar to "all arms" in modern English. The panoply itself refers to the entire set of all of the pieces of armor that compose the full set of armor for the Hoplite. It equates to a heavy-armed soldier or heavy infantry. The complete panoply would include a helmet, breastplate, and greaves, along with a sword and shield and a lance. Contrary to popular belief, the primary weapon of the Hoplite was the lance, or spear, not the sword. The sword was mostly used as a backup or emergency weapon, only after the Hoplite's main weapon, the spear, was lost or broken.

Another military innovation that cannot be understated is the development and adoption of phalanx tactics in combat. This method of unit formation was used by Hoplite unities all throughout the Classical period of Ancient Greece. The first evidence that was have uncovered that shows this tactical method in use does not occur until around the middle of the seventh century BC.

In the world of naval military development, the trireme was first developed and implemented during the Archaic period. Up until the eighth century BC, ships warships that employed two banks of oars and oarsmen had commonly been used by Greek navies. By the seventh century BC, the three-banked trireme had become more popular and commonplace. In the middle of the seventh century BC, Corinth likely became the first place in Greece to adopt the trireme, but it wasn't until a hundred years later that it became the most popular battleship design.

Chapter 3: Classical Greece

The period of time that we now refer to as the Classical Greece period was the era in Greek culture that spanned for in and around two hundred years between the fifth and fourth centuries BC. During this very historically important and significant period of time, Ancient Greece suffered the annexation of much of the territory that is currently sovereign to modern-day Greece by the great Persian Empire. After a period of foreign occupation, this same territory later became independent once more. This era of Classical Greece became a massive and strong influence on the Roman Empire. The Roman Empire would soon begin to rise as well as the large majority of western civilization all the way through subsequent history even up until this very day.

Modern politics in the west, with the artistic thought such as architecture and sculpture, philosophy, literature, theatre, and scientific concepts are derived and defined by the culture, developments, and ideologies of this period of time in Ancient Greece.

The most commonly cited events used as time markers for which to define the Classical period of Ancient Greece begin with the fall of the final tyrant in Athens in the year 510 BC and end with the death of Alexander the Great in the year 323 BC. This corresponds roughly to the fifth and fourth centuries BC. In the context of the culture, art, and architecture of Ancient Greece, these two centuries define the Classical period. Therefore by this reckoning, the Classical period of Ancient Greece comes immediately after the Archaic period and the Hellenistic period.

The Fifth Century BC

Beginning in the fifth century BC, in other words, the earliest years of Classical Greece culture, until approximately the end of the fifth century BC, which would correspond roughly to the mid-point of the Classical period, much of the academic study pertaining to Ancient Greece is examined through the lens of the Athenians. Athens of this time period has provided us the most plays, narratives, and other written documents, records and works of any of the Ancient Greek city-states.

The period that our modern times refer to as the fifth century BC extends, a small amount, into the fourth century BC because the calendar of the time was vastly different than that of ours today. By looking at it from this point of view, we could consider the first major event of that century to be the Cleisthenes' reforms. These events occurred following the fall of the last tyrant in Athens, during the year 508 BC. However, from a wider perspective of the entire Greek world of its Classical era, it could be argued that the beginning could be the Ionian Revolt with took place in the year 500 BC. This is the event that caused the first Persian invasion which happened in 492 BC. Persians would come to dominate much of the political and military worlds of Ancient Greece during the entire Classical era.

At the very beginning of the Classical era of Ancient Greece, Spartan soldiers assisted the Athenians in overthrowing their king, the tyrant known as Hippias, son of Peisistratos. The king of Sparta at the time, Cleomenes I, installed a pro-Spartan oligarchy in the city-state lead by Isagoras. However, Cleomenes I had a rival, Cleisthenes. Cleisthenes secured the support from the middle class and at the same time was helped by Democrats. With this strategic support and assistance, Cleisthenes was able to take control of the city. Cleomenes I tried to prevent the takeover from occurring at various periods in between the year 508 BC and the year 506 BC, but he was not able to prevent Cleisthenes from keeping control as he gained the full support of the Athenians.

The changes during this time came to be known as the Cleisthenes' reforms. Through these reforms, the people of Athens were able to endow their city with isotonic institutions. Isotonic institutions in this context refer to equal rights for citizens. Equal rights for all citizens were indeed implemented under the Cleisthenes' reforms, although it is important to note that these reforms were not truly an equally representative society, as only men were free citizens. The reforms set in place by Cleisthenes also established ostracism as a form of punishment and deterrence for the people of Athens. Ostracism was a custom and practice through which an Athenian citizen could be exiled for ten years from the city-state of Athens. It was often used as a pre-emptive measure to prevent a citizen who may have been perceived as being overly ambitious from rising to become a future tyrant.

While Greece was a major cultural, economic and geopolitical power during the Classical period, it was by certainly not the only powerful political entity on the world stage. To their east, gradually gaining power and dominance, was the Persian Empire. Even by the middle of the sixth century BC, the Persian Empire had begun to exert its control over neighboring Greece. The city-states in the region of Ionia, now located at the Aegean coast of modern Turkey, were unable to remain independent under the pressure of the encroaching Persian Empire and eventually came under their rule.

Eventually, in the year 499 BC, the Greek population of the Ionian region rose up against their Persian occupiers in what became known as the Ionian Revolt. A few other Greek city-states sent assistance to the cause. These events began the Battle of Lade in the year 494 BC. The Greeks were defeated and forced out of Ionia. After this significant Greek defeat, the entire region of Ancient Asia Minor returned to the control of the Persian Empire.

By the end of the first decade of the fifth century BC, the Persian Empire had subjugated Thrace and conquered Macedonia. A successful naval campaign in the Aegean Sea was also led at this time.

In the year 490 BC, the man who would eventually become quite possibly the most famous of the Persian Emperors, Darius the Great, sent a fleet of Persian warships to punish the Greeks. Darius the Great's army intended to take Athens by landing in Attica, but in the battle that ensued, the Battle of Marathon, the Persian army was soundly defeated by the general Miltiades of Athens. The Greek army had 1,000 Plataeans and 9,000 Athenian hoplites. The survivors of the Persian fleet moved on to Athens. Since Athens was strongly garrisoned, the Persians chose to call of any attempt at an assault.

Darius the Great was succeeded by Xerxes I. In the year 480 BC, the new king sent a much stronger force of some three hundred thousand soldiers by land with the support of 1,207 battleships across the Hellespont by means of a double pontoon bridge. The Persian army took over Thrace and then continued on to Thessaly and Boeotia, while the Persian navy ran interference and attempted to blockade the waterway.

King Leonidas I, the king of Sparta during the Agiad Dynasty, was able to delay the Persian army at the famous Battle of Thermopylae. In this legendary battle, three hundred Spartan soldiers went up against the entire Persian army. However, despite fighting bravely and giving their lives to slow down Xerxes I and his army, the Persians were still able to advance on Attica. Soon after, they captured and set fire to Athens, razing it to the ground. The majority of mainland Greece, just about every city-state north of the Isthmus of Corinth, had fallen to Persian control. Favorably, prior to the Battle of Thermopylae, the Athenians had been wisely evacuated from the city by means of the sea. Commanded by the great general Themistocles, Athens was able to secure a major turning point in the war with the defeat the Persian fleet at the Battle of Salamis.

By the year 483 BC, Greece was right in the middle of a time of peace in between the two Persian invasions. During this time, in a small, rural area in the vicinity of the city-state of Athens, a rich vein of silver ore was discovered. The vast wealth from this discovery was used in order to build some two hundred battleships that would be used to combat piracy in the Aegean Sea. The next year, under the command of the Spartans, the Greeks were able to defeat the Persian army. The Persian forces retreat from Greece and they would never again attempt another invasion.

Shortly after the Persian Invasions, Athens put it upon itself to unify the Greek city-states into an alliance that came to be called the Delian League. Sparta did not participate in this alliance and went into isolation. Athens became the most powerful commercial and naval power among the Classical Greek city-states.

During the latter half of the fifth century BC, the Classical Greek world had essentially split into two rival leagues or coalitions of Greek city-states. The first and ostensibly most powerful was the Delian League which centered on Athens. The rival league of Greek city-states began to arise which was centered on Sparta. As the threat from their neighbors in the Persian Empire began to subside, this coalition became more and more important. This Spartan league in known now as the Peloponnesian League.

There had been city-state coalitions in Greece in the past, including the Hellenic League, and well as the contemporary Delian League. These previously established coalitions had been formed in response to some form of external threat. The Peloponnesian League, on the other hand, existed for the sole and explicit purpose of putting strength and muscle behind Spartan policy. Its intention is to exert dominance and influence over the entire Peloponnese (a region in southern Greece) Peninsula. As these two internal powers jockeyed for dominance, the relations between them eventually deteriorated to the point of the war. This war is known today as the Peloponnesian War.

The initial strategy of Sparta in the opening stages of the Peloponnesian war was to take Attica by invasion. However, the Athenians managed to retreat and take shelter behind their walls. They were safe from the Spartan invaders behind their walls but an unexpected enemy reared its head in the form of a plague. The outbreak killed many people including the great general and orator, Pericles. After a few years of inconclusive fighting, a temporary peace was declared.

Hostilities were resumed, however, some years later, in the year 418 BC, after a conflict between Argos, an ally of Athens, and Sparta led to another full-scale war. After several more years of conflict all throughout the Ancient Greek world, the Peloponnesian War finally began to wind down at the end of the fifth century BC. Athens eventually was faced with bankruptcy after losing her entire fleet. The Spartans, on the other hand, received assistance from Persian. Athens demanded peace and despite the harsh settlement demands from Sparta, peace was declared.

The Fourth Century BC

As we roll into the fourth century BC in Classical Greece, we see the Peloponnesian War had left Sparta as the undisputed master of Greece. However, the Spartan mentality and culture of warrior elitism did not lend well to this particular role. After only a short number of years, the Democratic Party had already begun to regain power within Athens and in other city-states throughout Ancient Greece. By the year 395 BC rulers in Sparta had removed their naval commander from office, and the naval supremacy was now lost. Again, Sparta's superiority was challenged by Athens, Thebes, Argos, and Corinth, though these last two were former allies to Sparta, in what came to be known as the Corinthian War. The war ended in the year 387 BC without no decisive victor. Before long though, the powers were gathering against Sparta once more. Sparta chose to end the Treaty of Antalcidas with Persia. The unexpected decision to end this treaty, as part of the agreement therein, involved Sparta turning over Ionia and Cyprus back to Persia not considering the centuries of Greek combat against Persia on behalf of those cities. This decision led to more city-states uniting against Sparta.

The Peloponnesian War turned out to be a major turning point in the world of Ancient Greece. Over the next few decades, Greece descended into a complex series of power grabs. All of the major players vied for dominance. All attempted to establish their respective city-state into an empire in its own right. The Spartans, the Athenians, the Thebans, and the Macedonians all make attempts at Greek dominance during the entire fourth century BC.

The first of these city-states to establish itself as a legitimate city-state-empire was Sparta. While they were able to exert a powerful dominance in the Classical Greek world, their dominance ended up being rather short-lived. Spartan military strength dropped steeply during their brief stint as an empire. In the end, they were unable to defend their own city from other city-states. By the year 378 BC, the city-state of Thebes had begun rather tired of Spartan control over them, and a popular uprising was instigated, and in the year 375 BC, the army of Thebes won a great victory over the Spartans, who had vastly superior numbers, at the Battle of Tegyra.

During this time, the military strength and authority of Thebes had grown so intensely in such a notably short amount of time, that Athens began to distrust the expand power Thebes was coming to have. Athens made the move to consolidate as much of her power as possible by forming the Athenian League for the second time. This growing powder keg finally exploded in the year 371 BC, when the Theban army and the Spartans Clashed in the Battle of Leuctra. The Thebes handed Sparta a decisive defeat. Sparta left the battlefield having lost a huge portion of its forces as well as four hundred of its two thousand citizen troops. This was a major turning point in the entire Greek history. The Theban victory at the Battle of Leuctra ended a very long stretch of extreme prestige and elitism of the Spartan military. Both the dominance of Sparta and its time hegemony had come to an end.

But despite Thebes being the victory in this watershed battle against Sparta, Thebes did not in fact gain hegemony in Classical Greece, but on the other hand, it was Athens that ended up securing hegemony and becoming dominant once again.

This then led to the period of time in which the second Athenian league became something of an Empire itself, exerting its hegemony over the other city-states of Greece. However, this new Athenian League didn't last very long either. In many ways, the second Athenian League only really existed to guard against Sparta. But now, with the fall of Sparta in the year 371 BC, the alliance lost its purpose for existing and fell to structural weakness. Without conflict with Sparta to fuel their Alliance, they lacked the means to achieve their most modest ambitions, let alone the lofty ones. They had a very difficult time to even finance their navy, without even taking into account the forces of their entire alliance, and as such, they were simply unable to defend themselves and their allies and were not able to stand up to any pressure from city-states outside the alliance.

From the year 360 BC onward, Athens began to lose what reputation it had, as the alliance began to fall apart and allied city-states began to secede from the alliance.

By the year 357 BC, this revolt against the Athenian League had spread, and Athens would be forced to go to war against its own allies. Eventually, as the tensions and conflict escalated, the neighboring Persian emperor intervened in the war on behalf of the city-states in revolt. The Persian Emperor made the demand of the Athenians that they recognize the independence of their allies. This ultimatum was served with a threat of invasion with two hundred triremes sailing against Athens if they did not comply. Athens was forced to leave both the war and the Confederacy, which only served to weaken the flagging city-state, and signaled the conclusion of Athenian hegemony in Classical Greece.

After another brief empiric rise and rule with Thebes taking a shot at hegemony, until the entire Greek world became eclipsed by Macedon, a major power on the rise, in the year 346 BC. With the rise of Macedon came the rise of one of the greatest and most enduring historical figures of all time, Alexander the Great.

Alexander the Great is a topic all to himself, and many books have been dedicated to him through the hundreds of years since his death, but needless to say, Alexander the Great's influence over Classic Greece was unprecedented and total. His father, Phillip the Second of Macedon, had the grand ambition of conquering the entire Greek world, although he died by an assassin's blade before he could see this ambition through. Alexander, however, took up his father's ambition and succeeded decisively.

Despite Alexander the Great's historical pedigree, however, his untimely death in the year 323 BC, at the age of just thirty-two, sent the Greek world back into chaos and fragmentation. With that, the Classical Greek period comes to an end.

Chapter 4: Hellenistic Greece

The Hellenistic period of Ancient Greek history roughly incorporates the time between when Alexander the Great died and concluded with the rise of the Roman Empire. In Ancient Greek, the word Hellas was the original name of Greece, and this is where the word Hellenistic can draw its lineage from.

This period is when the cultural influence of Greece as well as its power was at its zenith throughout the Mediterranean, as well as the rest of Europe, Western Asia, and Northern Africa. Considered as the golden age for Greece, the arts were flourishing along with theatre, literature, sciences, philosophy, mathematics, music, architecture, exploration, and all manner of other fields and disciplines. The Hellenistic period of Ancient Greek history is also considered to be one of acute transition and has even been associated with a time of degeneration and decadence, especially when compared to the relative period of enlightenment that was experienced during the Greek Classical period.

Many new and long-lasting cultural innovations were taking place during this period, including but certainly not limited to the rise of Alexandrian poetry, which is characterized by the influences from the Alexander the Great founded city of Alexandria. Also coming to prominence during this era was the concept of New Comedy, which developed all through the period of Macedonian rule. The Septuagint was written in this time, which is the earlier known Greek translation of the Hebrew Old Testament from the original language of Hebrew. Philosophy also saw a major renewal in development, with the emergence of both the Stoic and Epicurean school of philosophy, which both came into prominence during the Hellenistic period of Ancient Greece.

In the period, science in Greece was being advanced by the timeless, enduring works of the great mathematician Euclid. Important mathematical and scientific contributions were also developed by the no less talented and legendary polymath Archimedes.

The sphere of influence of the religious beliefs in Hellenistic Greece expanded and came to include new gods into their panthea, such as the Greco-Egyptian god Serapis or various eastern gods like Attis or Cybele. There was also a fair amount of cultural and religious exchange between Hellenistic culture and the Buddhism that was taking hold in Bactria as well as in the northwest of India at the time.

After the invasion and conquest of the Persian Empire by Alexander the Great in the year 330 BC, the Hellenistic kingdoms had been established all the way through the south-west areas of Asia. Included are the Seleucid Empire and the Kingdom of Pergamon, as well the north-east of Africa, where the Ptolemaic Kingdom was located, and finally South Asia, the area that included the Greco-Bactrian Kingdom and the Indo-

Greek Kingdom. Alexander the Great's rise, conquest, and demise had certainly made major and long-lasting changes to the makeup and composure of the Greek world. The effect spread into the Hellenistic period of Ancient Greece and continue to influence the Greek world as well as the world at large for centuries to come.

The power vacuum caused by Alexander the Great's unexpected death was settled by dividing the empire into several far-flung kingdoms. The Hellenistic period of Greece was a fresh wave of Greek settlers spreading and colonizing. New Greek kingdoms were established in far-off city-states in the areas of Africa and Asia. Naturally, the vast spread of Greek people came with it widespread export of Greek culture and language, the results of which persisted up until our very modern day. In return, the far-flung new realms of Greek influence also took into themselves a very large amount of influence from the people indigenous to the area.

This pattern of varying and diverse cultural exchange is the reason for strong Greek cultural influence. Hellenistic culture came to represent the Ancient Greek world fusing with the cultures of the Middle East, Southwest Asia, and the Near East. It became very common for a Greek city-state, kingdom or realm to adopt customs and practices into their own culture, whether for practical purposes, strategic purposes, or otherwise, and thus the broader Greek world became something of a cultural melting pot at this period in time. This cultural and linguistic mixing also served to establish and spread new dialects of the Ancient Greek language. An example would be the Attic-based dialect that came to be known as Koine Greek, which is also known as Biblical Greek. It became the dominant trade language of the entire Hellenistic world.

There is no clear consensus among historians and Greek scholars as to what particular date or event marks the conclusion of the Hellenistic era of Ancient Greece. Several events have been put forward or have historically thought as the ending point of the Hellenistic world. The first such event would be the final and complete conquest of the primary heartlands of Greece by the Romans, which took place after the Achaean War in the year 146 BC. Another date proposed as an appropriate for the Hellenistic era of Greece is the final defeat and end of the Ptolemaic line of Kings, which occurred following the Battle of Actium in the year 31 BC. While other historians have even gone so far as to put forward that the Hellenistic era of Ancient Greece lasted all the up until the famous moving of the capital city of the Roman Empire from Rome to Constantinople by the Roman emperor Constantine the Great which happens centuries later in the year 330 AD.

The Diadochi

On June the 10th of the year 323 BC, Alexander the Great died, young and unexpectedly. Upon his untimely death, he left behind a massive empire which had been made up of the vast swaths of lands, territories, cities, and city-states that had been conquered during the famous and unprecedented campaigns of Alexander the Great. To govern and maintain such a vast empire, many of these territories and lands were made to be autonomous, self-governed regions which were known as satrapies. However, at the time of the death of Alexander the Great, he had not selected a successor to take up his rulership, the entire empire immediately plunged into a dispute between his generals to determine who should be the next king.

The wars of succession that came out of this chaotic state of affairs became known as the Diadochi wars, the first one which broke out shortly after the death of Alexander the Great.

Ultimately there were three wars of the Diadochi that saw conflict all throughout the Eastern Mediterranean, Northern Africa, and as the Far East and modern-day Northern India. By the end of the wars of the Diadochi, the power balance that would be maintained for much of the Hellenistic Period of Ancient Greece was in place. There were three territorial division that made up the primary power structure of the Hellenistic age, with the first being Macedon, which at this time was under the control of Antigonus II Gonatas. The second was the Ptolemaic kingdom in Egypt which was under the rule of Ptolemy I, who had advanced quite considerably in age at this point in history. And finally, the third major power in of the Hellenistic age of Greece was the Seleucid Empire, which at this point in time was now ruled by the son of its founder Seleucus, Antiochus I Soter.

These wars of the Diadochi lasted until the end of the third war in the year 275 BC. The wars saw the fall of two once influential Macedonian dynasties, the Antipatrid and the Argead dynasties, which the Antigonus dynasty taking power in their stead. This era in the history of Greece and Macedonia also is notable for the successive wars that took place between the one-time allies of Macedon, the Aetolian League and the Achaean League, and the Kingdom of Macedonia itself.

Between the years of 221 BC and 179 BC, which was during the rulership of King Philip V of Macedon, the empire of Macedonia suffered significant military and political setbacks. First of all, they were defeated in the Cretan War, which took place between the years of 205 BC and 200 BC, by the forces of Rhodesia and its allies. And then secondly, the alliance with Carthage that was set out in the Macedonia-Carthaginian Treaty of the year 216 BC, drew Macedonia into a conflict with early Ancient Rome, a power on the rise, in what become known as the First Macedonian War, which took place between the years of 214 BC and 205 BC. Soon after which was followed by the Second Macedonia War, which took place not long after the first one, between the years of 200 BC and 197 BC.

In the aftermath of these wars and conflicts, Macedonia came to be perceived as being weak and vulnerable. This negative perception led the Seleucid Empire under the rule of Antiochus III the Great to invade mainland Greece, however, this decision would eventually backfire on Antiochus III the Great, and set off a chain reaction of events that eventually put Rome in a position of military dominance in the entire area.

It is important to note that during the Hellenistic period of Ancient Greece, the importance of the region properly known as Greece, and the historic Greek city-states declined considerably amongst the entire Greek-speaking world. During this time, the major centers of culture in the Hellenistic period and region where the cities of Antioch and Alexandria, which were the capitals of the Syrian Seleucid Empire and Ptolemaic Egypt, respectively. However, many other cities became important hubs of culture, art, ideas and so forth, and indeed, the increasing urbanization of the entire Hellenistic region of the Eastern Mediterranean was a particularly notably facet of this time period in history.

The Rise of Rome

In the year 192 BC, tensions between the rapidly developing Rome and the ruler of the Seleucid Empire, Antiochus III, boiled over into full-scale war. At this time, Greece was invaded by Antiochus III with a force of someone in the neighborhood of ten thousand men. He was also elected to the position of the commander in chief of the alliance led by the Aetolians. To the cities and city-states in the Greek world, it was unclear which side of this conflict had their best interest in mind, but many of them felt that Antiochus III would be their savior and protect them from Roman occupation and oppression. Macedon, however, decided that it would lend its support to Rome, as they felt that Rome was the way of the future.

In the year 191 BC, the Roman general Marius Acilius Glabrio forced Antiochus III to withdraw from Greece and into Asia, after the Roman forces routed Antiochus at Thermopylae (not to be confused with the Battle of Thermopylae some three hundred years earlier in which three hundred Spartan led by King Leonidas held back the entire invading Persian army at the Hot Gates, during the Classical period of Ancient Greece). It was during this military engagement that the Roman army moved for the first time into Asia, pursuing Antiochus III and defeating him once again in the year 190 BC, in the battle of Magnesia at Magnesia ad Sipylum.

By this time, the Greek world was right in the middle of Rome proper, and the territories that Rome was invading and conquering. This meant that during this period, the Roman army was a constant and more or less permanent fixture in the Greek world. In the year 188 BC, the Peace of Apamaea was declared, which put Rome in a position of unrivaled dominance throughout Greece.

Throughout the following years, as Rome became more and more entrenched in their role, they were drawn deeper and further into Greek politics, by virtue of the fact that any time there was to be any kind of dispute of conflict, the defeated party would seek help from Rome. While Macedon was generally amenable to being an ally of Rome, they did nevertheless maintain their independence.

In the year 179 BC, Philip V died and his son Perseus succeeded him. Perseus, much like all of the many Macedonian rulers before him, wished to unite all Greek-speaking peoples and territories under one rule, the rule of Macedon. Unfortunately for Perseus, Macedon by this stage in history was far too weak and diminished to attain this goal. Nevertheless, an ally to Rome, Eumenes II of Pergamum, led Rome to believe that Perseus and Macedonia was a dire threat to Rome and that they would be wise to act or face destruction.

As a result of this pattern of rumor-mongering on the part of Eumenes II of Pergamum, in the year 171 BC, the great city of Rome declared all-out war on Macedon. In a bid for an advantage against what it had been lead to believe were vastly superior numbers, Rome rallied one hundred thousand troops and mobilized them into Greece. As it turned out, this massive Roman army was far larger than Perseus could have ever hoped to beat, and the rest of the neighboring cities and city-states were unwilling or unable to rally to their aid.

Rome was not yet the military juggernaut that it would become at its height under such men as Julius Caesar, Pompey the Great and others. As such, their generals at this time were prone to mistakes and miscalculations, and this siege was no exception. On account of this sub-standard leadership on the part of the Romans, Perseus and his forces were able to weather the siege for three years. In the year 168 BC, however, the Romans grew tired of the siege and sent the noted general Lucius Aemilius Paullus into Greece, where he took Macedon to task and dealt them a devastating and sound defeat at the first Battle of Pydna.

As a result of this crushing defeat, the Romans were able to capture Perseus, after which they took him to Rome. As a punitive measure, Rome then split up the kingdom of Macedonia into four individual and distinct states. At the same time, any and all Greek cities or city-states that Rome perceived to have aided or assisted the Macedonian kingdom, even in a passive way, were harshly punished as a means to deter future rebellions. Even two of Rome's allies, Pergamum and Rhodes, were punished and essentially lost their independence at this time.

Some years later, in the year 149 BC, a traveling adventurer, claiming to be the son of Perseus, lead Macedon into a rebellion in opposition to Roman rule. However, this was a clumsy and foolhardy endeavor, and the short-lived rebellion was crushed thoroughly. As a result of this failed effort, Macedon was annexed directly and became relegated to a subservient role as a Roman province.

With Rome now motivated and spurred on to crush and suppress any potential uprising or threat to its dominance, it moved to deliver the final blow to Greek independence. Rome demanded the surrender and dissolution of the Achaean League, which was the last true body of Greek independence and strength. Unsurprisingly, the Achaean League decline to dissolve themselves, and formally declared war on Rome, feeling that if they were going to be destroyed and subjugated, they would prefer to fight and die. The majority of the Greek cities chose to aid and assist the Achaean League and rallied in their support. Stories tell us of even slaves be freed en masse in order to fight for an independent Greece. The Roman consul at this time, Lucius Mummius, brought his army from Macedonia and advanced on Greece, defeating them at Corinth. He and his army then razed the Greek city to the ground.

Finally, in the year 88 BC, the King of Pontus, Mithridates the Great, was the last Greek ruler to rebel against Rome in the Ancient era. He raised an army and rode across Asia Minor, slaughtering upwards of one hundred thousand Romans as well as the allies of Rome. Even though Mithridates was himself not Greek, several Greek cities nevertheless rallied around him, including Athens, and they revolted and overthrew their leaders, who were puppets that had been installed by Rome.

Later, however, Mithridates the Great was once and for all driven away from Greece by the famed general Lucius Cornelius Sulla of Rome. After which, the vengeance of Rome once again befell the Greek world. Mithridates the Great was himself was not finally defeated until the year 65 BC, in which he was at last defeated in battle by one of the most prominent generals of the Late Roman Republic, Gnaeus Pompeius Magnus, who was also known as Pompey the Great.

Later on, Greece saw further ruin and destruction at the hands of Rome during the Roman civil wars, some of the battle of which took place in Greek territories. At last, in the year 27 BC, the first emperor of the newly formed Roman Empire, Augustus annexed Greece directly to the Roman Empire and gave them the name the province of Achaea. Much of the lands and territories of Greece were demoralized and depopulated by this point, on account of their struggles and conflicts with Rome. However, several cities, such as Corinth and Thessaloniki, and Athens were able to recover their prosperity and relative status after not too long, on account of the Pax Romana, the period of peace that came with the consolidation of power by the Roman Empire.

Chapter 5: Roman Greece

The Roman era of Ancient Greece refers to the period when the Roman Republic dominated the region, and eventually the Byzantine Empire. Collectively, these structures of Roman governance are referred to as the Roman era.

Ancient Greece under Roman rule began with the Corinthian's defeat against Rome in the Battle of Corinth, which took place in the year 146 BC. While that victory was indeed the beginning of the Roman supremacy of the Greeks, Rome did not definitely occupy the Greek world until the Battle of Actium, which took place in the year 31 BC. This was the great, historic battle in which the man who would become the first emperor of the new Roman Republic, Augustus, defeated his Greek foes, the Ptolemaic Greek Queen Cleopatra VII, and her general and lover, Mark Antony. The following year, Augustus proceeded to take over Alexandria, which at the time was the last true center of Hellenistic Greek culture.

The Greek world stayed under Roman rule for hundreds of years, all the up until the year 330 AD, when the great Empire of Rome went on to adopt the city of Byzantium as Nova Roma, the new capital of the Roman Empire. At this stage in history and afterward, the Eastern Roman Empire shifted into a mostly Greek-speaking territory.

Early Roman History

The geological feature described as the Greek peninsula first fell to Roman rule in the year 146 BC. This change in rulership was the result of the Battle of Corinth. The Battle of Corinth was the major conflict between Rome and Macedonia in which Rome was victorious and Macedonia became a province of

Rome after it was directly annexed by the Roman republic. At this same time, on account of a newly bred mistrust for the Greek land and territories, Macedonia's new Roman appointed prefect carefully and cautiously surveilled the rest of southern Greece.

Some of the more cunning and willful of the Greek poleis were able to generally avoid taxes, and largely maintain some degree of at least partial independence. In the year 133 BC, the King Attalus III passed away. This was significant for two reasons. The reason it was significant is on account of the fact that he was the ruler of the Kingdom of Pergamon, which at this time was relatively independent of Roman rule, although it was heavily pressured by Rome and very much under Roman influence. The second reason as to the significance of King Attalus II's passing of the Kingdom of Pergamon was because in his final will and testament, he had left his kingdom and his territories to the people of Rome. This act resulted in the Kingdom of Pergamon effectively being incorporated into the Roman territories.

But while this convenient bequest was a boon for Rome, they were not quick to secure their claim over their new territories. During this time a pretender to the throne of the kingdom of Pergamon, going by the name of Aristonicus, rallied a revolution with the assistance of the stoic philosopher and revolutionary Blossius.

That uprising was expectedly put down in the year 129 BC, at which point the former kingdom of Pergamon was dissolved and its territories were divided and shared between Rome, Cappadocia, and Pontus. Later on, in the year 88 BC, Athens revolted with the aid and assistance of several other Greek cities. That popular uprising was also quickly and relatively easily crushed by the highly effective and celebrated Roman general Sulla.

A few decades later, as the Roman Republic collapsed under its own weight and descended into civil war, the lands and territories suffered even further, as the wars and conflicts of Rome continued to devastate the land. Finally, in the year 27 BC, the brand new emperor of the newly-minted Roman Republic consolidated the entire Greek peninsula and organized it as a province under the name of Achaea.

The lands and cities of Greece were absolutely devastated economically by these turbulent and disruptive events. However, after the Roman civil wars came to an end, the economies of these cities and lands began to rise back up dramatically. The Greek cities that were located in the region of Asia Minor generally recovered in earlier and faster than the cities and lands of the Greek peninsula proper. This was very likely on account of the fact that the cities located on the peninsula had seen more and heavier damage by General Sulla's Roman forces, then had the cities throughout the lands of Asia Minor.

But in the years that followed, the Romans sunk some very heavy investment funds into these cities for the purpose of rebuilding them and getting them into a state of growth and prosperity once again. For the newly declared province of Achaea, the city of Corinth was decided on to be the new capital city. And while Athens was not as politically or militarily dominant as it once had been, it went on to see continued prosperity as a hub of learning and philosophy throughout the Greek, and now Roman, world.

The Early Roman Empire

Under the rule of the new Roman Empire, the life of most people in the lands of the Greek world continue more or less the way it had previously, only under a different rule and with different leaders. But by and large, the culture of Rome was more likely to be influenced by Greece, than for Greek culture to be influenced by Rome. Much of the culture and beliefs of Rome during this time were in fact very highly influenced by the culture and lives of the Greek people. Much of the Roman Empire arts and literature were also inspired and otherwise influenced by the arts and literature of Greece both contemporary and historical. One particularly notable example of such cultural borrowing by means of arts and literature is that of the *Aeneid* of Virgil, which was noticeably inspired by the epic works of the Greek poet Homer. Similarly, many works of Roman writing during this time were indeed written in imitation of the Greek style by their Roman authors, such as, for example, the works of the author and philosopher Seneca the younger.

While it is certainly true that not all Roman nobles valued the Greeks or Greek culture, many of them looked down on the Greek people as being backward or uncivilized. At the same time, a great many of the Roman nobles, many of them went on to quite an enormous deal of fame and fortune, duly embraced the philosophies and literature of the Greeks. The Greek language went on to become the primary language of the elite and the highly educated in Rome. One important and particularly notable example of this Roman embrace of the Greek language and culture was that of the great general Scipio Africanus, who is considered to be one of, if not singularly the greatest military commander, tactician and strategist to have ever lived, often being mentioned in the same sentences as Alexander the Great, Julius Caesar and Napoleon Bonaparte.

Scipio Africanus studied a great deal of philosophy, and he considered the culture and science of the Greeks to be an example that should be followed.

After a similar fashion, most of the emperors who ruled over the duration of the Roman Empire tended to admire and respect Greek culture and generally all things that had a Greek origin or a Greek nature. An excellent example of one such Roman emperor with a strong passion for Greek culture was that of Roman Emperor Nero. In the year 66 AD, the Roman Emperor Nero went to Greece for a visit and for the Ancient Olympic Games. Emperor Nero, to everyone's surprise, actually performed in the games, despite that fact the rules for the Ancient Olympic Games prohibited anyone who was not Greek from participation. The Greeks honored him by proclaiming him the victor in every contest. Emperor Nero returned the honor in the year that followed, at the Isthmian Games in Corinth, where he proclaimed the freedom of all Greeks, just as had done Flamininus some two hundred years prior to this. It has also been noted that the emperor Hadrian was rather quite fond of the Greeks and of their culture. He commissioned the building of the arch that bears his name, the Arch of Hadrian in Athens, which happens to be the city where he served as an eponymous archon prior to becoming the Emperor of the Roman Empire.

As a matter of fact, many of the public buildings and temples that were built in the Greek cities during this period were specifically commissioned by the emperors and the wealthy class of elite Roman nobility. This fact is particularly true of the city of Athens. In fact, one of the more famous buildings in Athens, the Roman Agora, was commissioned by Julius Caesar himself, although it wasn't completed until after his death, by Augustus. The primary gate of this structure, the Gate of Athena Archegetis, was dedicated to Athena, the patron goddess of Athens. In the center of this freshly built Roman Agora was built the Agrippina, by Marcus Vipsanius Agrippa.

In the year 50 BC, Andronicus of Cyrrhus built the Tower of the Winds, however, it is possible that this structure may actually predate the Roman portion of Athens in its entirety. In a very similar fashion, the Roman emperor Hadrian was also a very strong admirer of the Greeks and of Greek culture. It is suggested that he even considered himself to be an heir to Pericles, and as such he as well made numerous contributions to the city of Athens.

One of these numerous contributions made to Athens by Hadrian was the Library of Hadrian. Another particularly notable contribution and accomplishment on the part of emperor Hadrian to Athens was his completion of the Temple of Olympian Zeus, a temple so massive and imposing that construction on it had begun some six hundred and thirty-eight years before its completion by the tyrants of Athens during the Age of the Tyrants in the Archaic era of Ancient Greece. At that time, the construction of the Temple had been abandoned as it was believed that to attempt the construction of a building on such an enormous scale would appear to be hubristic before the gods.

After the construction of this remarkable Temple of Olympian Zeus was completed, the people of Athens showed their gratitude to the emperor who contributed so much to their city by commissioning the construction of the Arch of Hadrian in honor of the emperor Hadrian. Leading away from the Arch of Hadrian, in the direction of the Roman Agora, to this day exists Hadrian Street.

With the establishment of the Roman Empire, a period of comparative stability and peace followed in its wake. This time period is referred to as the Pax Romana. In the entire course of Greek history up until that point, the Pax Romana represented the longest period of peace Greece had ever seen. During this period, Greece also became an essential crossroads for the trade network by land and sea between the city of Rome itself, and the eastern territories of the Roman Empire, which were still largely Greek-speaking by this point in time. The language of Greece too was still highly crucial to the success of the Roman Empire, as it became not only the primary trade language and bridge language for the Empire, but the Greek language was also taken up by Roman elites. To complete this pattern of cultural exchange, even many Greek scholars and intellectuals did much if not most of their work within the city of Rome.

In the earliest decades of the Roman Empire and of the Roman Empire's rule over Greece, Early Christianity grew stronger and more powerful throughout both the Greek world and throughout the entire Roman Empire. Saul of Tarsus, who was more well-known by his Christian as the Apostle Paul, made several preaching campaigns around the Mediterranean, including Athens, Corinth, and Philippi. Before long, the Greek world became more Christianized than almost any other part of the entire Roman Empire.

Late Roman Empire

Later on in the history of the Greek and Roman worlds, namely, during the second and third centuries AD, Greece had been divided into several distinct provinces, including Macedonia, Achaea, Thrace, and Epirus. During the last years of the third century AD, as part of the reign of Diocletian, Moesia came to be organized into a diocese, which was under the rule of Galerius. Under the rule of Emperor Constantine, the first Roman Emperor to convert to Christianity, and then declare Rome to be a Christian Empire, Greece came to be governed under the prefectures of Thrace and Macedonia. Later, Roman Emperor Theodosius further split up the prefecture in Macedon into six smaller provinces. These were Macedonia, Epirus Nova, Epirus Vetus, Thessalia, Achaea and finally Creta. Meanwhile, the Aegean islands made up the province of Insulae, which was part of the Diocese of Asia.

During the period of history which corresponds to the reign of Romulus Augustulus, Greece was forced to face down several different invasions, perpetrated by the Vandals, the Goths, and Heruli. In the later period of the fourth century AD, a man named Stilicho, assumed the role of ruler of the land on behalf of the real ruler Arcadius, under false and duplicitous pretenses. He was a general of the Roman army who was of a particularly notably high rank. But while he was half Vandal, he was married to the young woman who happened to be the niece of Emperor Theodosius I, and as such was able to secure for himself a high degree of respect and responsibility within the Roman army. But while this was most certainly a high water mark in terms of the advancement of members from within the Germanic or, Barbaric tribes, within the Roman army's command structure, Stilicho made the unpopular decision to evacuate Thessaly when the Visigoths invaded.

The Chief advisor for Arcadius, a man by the name of Eutropius, made a concession by allowing Alaric, the man who crowned himself the first King of the Visigoths, between the years of 395 AD and 410 Ad, to enter into Greek territory. In so doing, Alaric ransacked the lands of Greece and went through the territory, looting cities. One by one, cities fell throughout the lands of Ancient Greece. The city of Athens was looted. The city of Corinth was also thoroughly looted during this brutal campaign. And as well, the lands of the Peloponnese, already having been ruined by war and hardship for hundreds of years, was also entered, pillaged and looted for all it was worth.

The pretended named Stilicho was eventually able to mount a counter-offensive and pressed his men into service for the express purpose of removing King Alaric of the Visigoths out of Greece altogether. Eventually, in and around the year 397 AD, Stilicho was indeed able to drive Alaric out of Greece. Whether this whole episode was just the natural course of events, or whether it was some kind of elaborate ruse by the invading barbarians is unclear to this day, and was likely even less clear at the time, as these events were marked by secrecy, silence and cunning, but nevertheless, Alaric was named magister *militum* in the land of Illyricum. The position of magister *militum* was a very high levers military command post that was used prominently in the late Roman Empire, thought to have begun being implemented around the time of the Roman Emperor Constantine. Later though, after a short amount of time with Alaric using his position of magister *militum* for whatever purpose he may have taken it, he and the rest of the Goths moved on and migrated west toward Italy.

On the way, they managed to sack the great city of Rome. This monumental event in history happened in the year 410 AD. Later, as they continued to move west, they moved into the Iberian Peninsula and were able to build up the Visigothic Kingdom. This brand new kingdom made up of what the Romans considered to be barbarians ended up enduring for hundreds of years and lasted all the way until sometime in the year 711 AD when the Arabs arrived and were able to wrest control from the Visigoths.

The eastern half of the now divided Roman Empire commonly referred to as the Eastern Roman Empire, or the Byzantine Empire continued on with Greece remaining an important part of this relatively unified half of the Roman Empire in the east. While it was believed by historians for a long time that the Greek world suffered greatly during this time, it is now believed that the Greek peninsula was actually more likely to be rather prosperous during this time. In fact, it is likely that it was one of the most prosperous regions in all of the lands of the Roman Empire. More recent archaeological research has revealed that the polis system of city governance and wealth generation were still active and prosperous quite possibly all the way up to and into the sixth century AD.

We have even recovered contemporary texts written during this time, such as for example the *Syndekmos* of Hierokles, which show us that Greece during the late Antiquity was in fact very highly urbanized and had within its borders somewhere in the neighborhood of 80 cities. Today, in our modern era, the idea of Greece being extremely prosperous during late Antiquity is much more widely accepted. It is now believed that during in between the centuries of the fourth and seventh centuries AD, it is quite likely that Greece was one of the most economically successful regions of the Mediterranean in the east.

Chapter 6: The Byzantine Empire and the Greek Legacy

The lands of Greece and the entire Greek world had been under Roman rule for centuries now. As the Roman Empire itself began to fracture and weaken, tumultuous times would come with it. Eventually, the Roman Empire was split into two distinct empires, the Western Roman Empire and the Eastern Roman Empire. The Eastern Roman Empire would also be referred to as the Byzantine Empire.

Invasions and Changing Times

The lands of Greece fell within the boundaries of the Byzantine Empire. During the changing and shifting times of the early centuries of the Common Era, Greece largely changed and shifted with the times alongside the massive and still very powerful Byzantine Empire.

After Antioch and Alexandria fell to the Arabs, Thessaloniki became the second largest city in the Byzantine Empire, second only to Constantinople. Thessaloniki would then be declared the 'co-regent" alongside Constantinople. At this time, the Greek peninsula continued to be one of the biggest and strongest hubs of Christianity throughout the entire late Roman and well into the early Byzantine periods.

After having recovered from a number of invasions perpetrated by the Slavic peoples, the wealth of the Greek world was restored. Later on, as the Byzantine era progressed, certain events began to change the way the Byzantine Empire operated. Such notable events include the defeat and occupation of Constantinople by the Latin Empire of Romania, as well the invasion of Asia Minor by the Turko-Persian Seljuk

Empire. These particular events, along with many others, led the Byzantine Empire to turn its focus and interests toward the Greek peninsula. Despite this period of domination by the Latins to the recovery of the Byzantine Empire and all the way through the final fall of the Byzantine Empire to the Ottomans, the Peloponnese remained prosperous economically, although many others Greek cities were rather successful all through these changing eras as well.

By the time of the reign of the emperor Andronicus III Palaeologus, who took power over the Byzantine Empire in the year 1328 AD, the Byzantine Empire still had secure control over the majority of Greece. By this time the urban metropolis center of Thessalonians was of particular importance, and the Byzantine Empire controlled this region, but not a whole lot else. The land of Epirus was technically under Byzantine rule, but would still take any opportunity it could find to rebel, although it was finally recovered for good in the year 1339 AD.

Much like it had for hundreds of years, the lands of Greece were largely used as a battleground. It saw a large degree of the fighting during the civil war which occurred in the 1340s between John VI Cantacuzenus and John V Palaeologus. Meanwhile, at more or less the same period in time, the Ottomans and the Serbs began to attack the Greek lands.

Disease

The lands of the Peloponnese, which during this period of time became primarily known as the Morea, was, by and large, the epicenter of the Byzantine Empire and was definitely the most fertile and productive region. The cities of Monemvasia and Mystras were also rather prosperous and populous, although the Black Plague did a number on them in the middle of the 14th century. They were able to recover and remain successful and prosperous, however. During this time, Mystras even rivaled the great capital of Constantinople for a time in its importance. In this era, many emperors sought to unite the Empire with the Roman Catholic Church, which had gained incredible power and influence by this time, but the Greek lands were still a great stronghold for the Greek Orthodoxy, and they persistently and bitterly fought against these attempts, despite the fact that aligning with the Roman Catholic Church would have opened up the empire to assist from the west against the Ottoman Empire.

By this point in time, the Ottomans had begun their assault and conquest of the lands of Greece as well as the Balkans, which persisted and continued throughout the latter part of the 14th century AD and the earlier years of the 15th century AD. The future emperor Constantine XI, who at the time was a despotic ruler of the city of Mystras, managed to recapture the city of Thessaly from Ottoman occupation in the year 1445, although even with this victory, there was little that could be done in order to capture or reclaim the rest of the Ottoman territories. In the year 1453 AD, the Ottomans were finally able to capture the city of Constantinople, and with it, they captured and killed Emperor Constantine.

Constantine's death marked the fall of Constantinople. By the year 1458 AD, the Ottomans had also managed to capture the Aegean islands as well as the city of Athens. However, the Ottomans did leave a Byzantine despotate to rule the Peloponnese until the year 1460 AD. At this time, the Venetians still maintained control of the island of Crete as well as some Greek ports, but apart from that, the Ottomans were in control of many regions of Greece. However, the mountains and regions with heavy forestation remain free and under Greek control.

Final Thoughts

Thus, we come to an end of the 2000-year Greek saga that began all the way back in early antiquity by a civilization of people clawing their way out of a dark age. A people that would go on to build the foundation of democracy, art, science, and culture that persists well into this day, and has lasted through many, many empires, great and small. It has stood the test of time, and now to this day, the lands of the Greek nation and the historic locations and sights of this historically and cultural priceless land stand there for all who wish to take heed and notice. There is always much to be learned about history, and finding out about our ancestors will always play a vital role in our modern world.

Conclusion

You've made it through to the end of *Ancient Greece*! Let's hope it was informative and able to equip you with the knowledge and tools you need to.

The next step is to keep learning what you can about the Ancient World. Learning about history is one of the most important ways to gain insight into the world around us, and gives us an important lens through which to view our modern world. What's more, awareness of the mistakes and advances of the past will better equip us and our society for a better future.

In this book, we learned much about Greece in antiquity. We learned about the early rise to power of the Archaic Greek world as it rose out of the ashes of the old Mycenaean kingdom. We then dove into Classical Greece and the major developments that were made in the fields of politics, the arts as well as the military tactics and strategies that have made a massive impact on the world. The principles and concepts within these fields are still used both during contemporary times and equally, down to our today.

Moving past the classical period, we learned about the era of Hellenistic Greece when the makeup of the Greek world changed dramatically and spread throughout the then known world. Also, we learned about the rise of the City-States, such as Athens and Sparta, which would go on to be dominated by Macedon.

Finally, we dug deep into Greece under Roman rule, and how it went on to take its place in history as a land of cultural heritage that would have a significant and enduring legacy.

Ancient Rome

A Concise Overview of the Roman History and Mythology Including the Rise and Fall of the Roman Empire

Additionally, the contents of the following pages are intended only for informational purposes; thus, it should be thought of as universal. As befitting its nature, it is presented without assurance regarding its prolonged validity or interim quality. Trademarks that are mentioned are done without written consent and can in no way be considered an endorsement from the trademark holder.

Introduction

Few societies and historical periods capture our fascination as much as ancient Rome. With a founding steeped in legend, along with the rise and fall of a monarchy, a republic, and an empire filled with colorful, and often even bizarre, leaders and popular figures, it is no wonder that it has been the source of inspiration for a multitude of novels, movies, and television shows. While this entertainment fare has had varying degrees of historical accuracy, a great deal of artistic license does not need to be taken to make the story of ancient Rome intriguing and scintillating. It was a society and a people rich with drama that still captures our interest even today, more than 1500 years since the fall of the great Roman Empire.

There are many books on this subject on the market; nonetheless, thank you once again for choosing this one! Every effort was made to fill it with as much useful information as possible. Please enjoy!

Chapter 1: The Founding of Rome and Rise of a Republic

Remus and Romulus

The story of the founding of Rome is one steeped in legend and enough drama to rival any modern-day soap opera or novella. The mythology of its origin centers on the twin brothers, Romulus and Remus, who were known in various legends to be the sons of a mortal woman and either the god, Mars, or the demigod, Hercules. The woman, Rhea Silvia, was the daughter of Numitor, the deposed king of Alba Longa, a city in the central area of the Italian peninsula. Rhea Silva was forced to take vows of chastity as a Vestal Virgin, a priestess in service to the goddess of home and hearth, Vesta. This was to prevent her from producing heirs who might renew claims to the throne.

Fearing that the divinely conceived twins might become rivals for his title, the usurper king of Alba Longa, Amulius, who was also Rhea Silvia's uncle, ordered that the twin infants be killed. He stipulated that their murders should be through drowning, a method chosen to prevent possible retribution from the gods. Taking even further care to avoid having the blood of his kin on his hands, Amulius relegated the murderous task to a servant, who was instructed to cast the boys into the River Tiber. The servant was unable to carry out the task, however, taking pity on the infants. Instead, he sent them down the river in a basket.

Legend holds that the river god, Tiberinus, calmed the waters to ensure the twin's safe journey, and assisted in letting the basket reach the riverbank at the base of one of the Seven Hills of Rome, the Palatine. After washing ashore, they were found by a she-wolf, or Lupa, that suckled them. The animal kept them alive until they were discovered and taken in by a shepherd named Faustulus and his wife, Acca Larentia. The boys were raised by Faustulus as his own sons. They grew up to become shepherds, following in the footsteps of the man who adopted them.

There are several variations of the story on how the twins eventually discovered their true identities and confrontation that followed with Amulius, their great uncle and the still-sitting king who had ordered their deaths. Yet, all versions of the legend agree that Remus and Romulus killed Amulius. They then declined the offer to take the throne of Alba Longa, preferring instead to establish a new city and return the title back to their grandfather, Numitor.

Upon determining to found a new city of their own, the brothers argued about the appropriate location. Romulus believed that it should be at the site where they had washed ashore as infants, near the Palatine. Remus was of another mind, however, choosing to settle near another part of the Seven Hills, the Aventine. Unable to come to an agreement, they determined to leave the decision to the hands of the gods by seeking signs of prophecy in the natural world, a practice termed as augury.

Unfortunately, this also failed to settle the conflict, since they disagreed on the meaning and significance of the signs that they had seen. Refusing to remain at an impasse, Romulus decided to move forward with the construction of a new city at the Palatine even without his twin's assent. This further deepened the conflict between them. What began as a petty quarrel tragically ended in fratricide. Romulus killed his brother and crowned himself king of the new settlement. He called it *Roma*, or what we now know as "Rome," after his own name.

The Roman Monarchy (753 – 509 BCE)

Romulus' taking of the throne as the first king of the new city, which is understood as having been in 753 BCE, is acknowledged as the beginning of the Roman Monarchy. This was a period of nearly 250 years that was marked by the development of a new system of government, a number of unusual measures that were intended to increase the population of the city, and a series of conflicts and wars with neighboring cities and peoples.

The Senate

One of Romulus' innovations in government was the establishment of a 100-member Senate, or *senatus*. The literal meaning of the word, which was that of a "gathering of old men," indicates both its constitution and practical function in the monarchy. Consisting of individuals from the upper ranks of society and those with a great deal of experience in public service, the Senate primarily served in an advisory capacity to the city's elected officials called the magistrates. While the Senate was not empowered with law-making capacities, its guidance and decisions were highly influential in the adoption of new laws.

As a position in the Senate was a highly influential one, those who held the rank were entitled to certain practical and social privileges. These ranged from special financial opportunities and benefits to preferred seating at public events and the wearing of distinguished garments and accessories. A specific hue known as Tyrian purple was associated with royalty and the highest positions of honor in ancient Rome. It was a color that was difficult to produce for use in fabrics, with the extraction of its pigment requiring the use of thousands of a certain type of marine snail. The scarcity of the components and the complexity of the process of producing the color made it as one that denoted a high social rank. Senators were permitted to wear a strip of purple on their togas, and wore rings signifying their membership in the important government body.

The Senate could gather anywhere within the city or its immediate outskirts as long as the meeting place was deemed sacred such as a temple, or *templum*. They gathered most often in a public building known as the Curia. Its precise structure, however, changed over the years through the different periods of the monarchy, Republic, and Imperial Rome. The Curia was open to the public, as were the meetings. Anyone was allowed to attend, and people often did sit outside of the Curia to listen in on important and influential debates and discussions among the senators.

Yet even with the existence of a senate, most of the power and authority in the Roman monarchy rested in the hands of the king. The king had full control over law-making, political measures and policies, the appointment of public officials, and military activities and issues. He even had the final word in religious matters. Any dispute could be decided by the king, who was recognized as the final and ultimate authority.

Population Development

When Romulus founded Rome, he encouraged population growth by inviting and welcoming everyone who wished to become a resident of the city, no matter what sort of past that individual might have. Consequently, large numbers of people with criminal histories were attracted to Rome, as were former slaves and freemen, most of whom were male.

This open-door approach was extremely effective in boosting citizenship, and the population of Rome rapidly increased. This led to the necessity of expanding the city beyond its original site of the Palatine, to encompass three more of the other Seven Hills. One of these was Aventine, Remus' choice for the initial settlement.

The policy resulted in a population that was overwhelmingly male, which was not conducive to either a satisfied citizenry or to long-term population growth. In historical accounts of early Rome, it is said that Romulus initially tried to deal with this issue by negotiating with neighboring towns, cities, and societies, to encourage female members of their populations to marry Roman men.

When those negotiations proved unsuccessful, Romulus conceived a scheme to kidnap a large number of women from the Sabines, a group of people living in the central area of the Apennine Mountains. To achieve this desired end, Romulus planned an elaborate festival to honor the god, Neptune, and invited the residents of the surrounding areas to attend. It is said that at some point in the festival, the Sabine women were abducted while their male counterparts were attacked, killed, or driven off.

This event was known as "The Rape of the Sabine Women." The terminology has been subject to much debate, both historically and at the present day, with many holding that it was characterized by kidnapping and abduction, not assault. Yet one of the grounds upon which the Sabine women were enticed or coerced into marrying Roman men is recorded as having involved a plea for the "common children." The plea, purportedly delivered to all Sabine women individually by Romulus himself, suggested that many may have been impregnated during the time of their abduction.

Whatever the actual details may have been, the effort served to instigate the first of Rome's wars, fought against the Sabines, and from which Rome emerged victorious. After being defeated, the Sabines entered into a treaty with Rome, agreeing to the merging of their populations and to a joint rulership of the resultant society. This cooperative endeavor gave rise to a merging of cultures, with both peoples adopting each other's customs and practices. This is something that would come to characterize ancient Roman society throughout the full span of its existence.

As the population grew, Romulus divided his citizens into tribes based on their areas of origin and ethnicity. The Sabines represented one tribe, as did the Etruscans, with the third tribe being the Roman people. The post-treaty joint rulership with the Sabines brought five years of peace and relative harmony until the Sabine king, Tatius, sheltered and then freed criminal fugitives, leading to his assassination. Thus, Romulus was left as the sole king with full authority over the new, merged society.

The Passing of Romulus

For the following two decades, Rome continued to expand, increasing its territory and populace through war and, when Romulus' grandfather died, through inheritance. As Rome grew, so did the king's handle on power. While there is very little historical information that accurately recounts the factual events, it is commonly believed that Romulus' increasingly autocratic methods sparked resentment in the Senate, who begrudged the loss of their influence on public matters.

Some sources suggest that Romulus was ultimately assassinated by the Senate or by those operating under its instructions. Others assert that his demise was as divinely influenced as his conception, claiming that eyewitnesses have attested to the fact that he mysteriously disappeared during a storm that had interrupted a religious ceremony in 717 BCE. In some accounts, it is reported that he became a god upon his death. Such a report has contributed to speculation that the story of Romulus and his brother, Remus, was a myth, and not the history of actual men.

The Line of Kings

The Roman monarchy continued after Romulus' reign and death. Whether it was real or fable, his succession saw a series of kings with varying personalities and goals, each contributing to the growth and evolution of the city and culture of Rome.
A brief overview of the kings and some of their notable features and contributions:

Numa Pompilius

Years of rule: 715 - 673 BCE
Numa was a member of the Sabine tribe who was more interested in living a solitary life, studying religion and philosophy, than ruling. He reluctantly accepted the title of king; doing so only after consulting an augury to determine the wishes of the gods regarding his fate.
Known for:

- Adding January and February to the annual calendar, increasing the number of days in a year to 360.

- Relocating the order of priestesses of Vesta, the Vestal Virgins, from Alba Longa to Rome.

- Marking the borders of the Roman territory.

- Allotting land to farmers of the peasant class to ensure consistent food production and supply.

- Establishing an order of priests, the Fetiale collegium, to serve as ambassadors and advise the Senate on international treaties and measures of war and peace.

- Creating a role of a head priest to oversee all religious activities, called a *Pontifex Maximus*.

- Introducing professional guilds to Rome to alleviate tensions between the tribal groups.

Numa is recognized as having been a peaceful and thoughtful leader who initiated many institutions and practices that continued to live on long after his period of rule.

Tullus Hostilius

Years of rule: 673 - 641 BCE
Unlike his predecessor who was known as a man of peace, Tullus is characterized as a war hawk. He had little regard for the wishes of the gods; shunning religious ceremonies until a string of events transpired that caused him to become increasingly superstitious. Yet, like the first king of the monarchy, Romulus, many scholars question his existence as a real historical figure due to a number of inconsistencies in the work attributed to him.
Known for:

- Being warlike and consistently engaging in campaigns throughout his rule.

- Improving the organization of the Roman army.

- Incorporating Alba Longa into Rome.

- Establishing the *Curia Hostilia*, the first formal chamber for Senate meetings, which included an exterior area for citizens to meet and vote on public matters, the *Comitium*.

Along with other similarities to Romulus, it is said that Hostilius also died during a storm, allegedly struck down by a lightning bolt sent by the god, Jupiter.

Ancus Marcius

Years of rule: 641 -616 BCE
Grandson of the second king of Rome, Marcius is noted for having borne a number of similarities with Numa, including a peaceful agenda and a desire to improve matters related to Rome's cultural and social affairs.
Known for:

- Expanding Rome to encompass another of the Seven Hills, the Janiculum, to accommodate an ever-growing population, and for its strategic location.

- Establishing the coastal port of Ostia, improving access to trade with other cities, towns, and peoples of the Mediterranean.

Due to his likeness to Numa, Marcius was initially mistaken for being a weak king and consequently faced challenges that resulted in war. He ultimately proved himself to be a strong and capable military leader.

Lucius Tarquinius Priscus (Tarquin the Elder)

Years of rule: 616 - 579 BCE

Tarquin rose through the ranks of Roman political society and became a close ally of Marcius; even being named as guardian of his sons. While the hereditary rule was not yet in place during the monarchy, Tarquin feared that the kingship will go to Marcius' heirs upon his death. He successfully plotted to acquire the throne.

Known for:

- His plot to secure the throne from Marcius' sons.

- Making many reforms to the Roman army, such as increasing the size of the cavalry.

- Introducing a number of Etruscan elements into the symbols and insignia associated with the Roman throne.

Tarquin's plotting against Marcius' sons for possession of the throne eventually caught up with him, as they ultimately hired assassins to kill him with the blow of an ax. His wife and his adopted son (some sources define him as a close friend), Servius Tullius, hid his death from the people. Servius then established himself as an interim ruler while Tarquin purportedly recovered from his wounds. When the truth about his death finally came to light, Servius had served long enough to be proven a competent leader, and his claim to the throne was unchallenged.

Servius Tullius

Years of rule: 579 - 535 BCE

Servius was believed by many in Rome to have been in line for a great destiny since the time of his infancy, when it was reported that a ring of fire appeared around his head, while the rest of his body remained unharmed. He aligned himself with

Tarquin the Elder, which resulted in his ascension to the throne after the king's death. His claim was further strengthened by the marriage of his two daughters to Tarquin's two sons.

Known for:

- Having such a resounding triumph over Etruscan forces in battle, that he was able to avoid another war for the rest of his reign, which lasted 44 years.

- Introducing a census.

- Extending voting rights to certain classes of common, or lower, citizens.

- Creating tensions between the upper and lower classes, the Patricians and the Plebeians, by making decisions favorable to the latter.

The conflicts that arose from Servius' activities and actions that favored the lower classes, combined with the somewhat questionable way in which he had gained the throne, compelled his youngest daughter to conspire with Tarquin's son, Lucius Tarquinius. They arranged for his murder, which occurred on the steps of the Curia.

Lucius Tarquinius Superbus (Tarquin the Proud)

Years of rule: 534 - 509 BCE

After conspiring in the death of Servius, Lucius claimed the throne as the last of the kings of the monarchy. He earned the suffix of "Superbus," which translates to "arrogant," due to his personality and the ruthlessness of his actions in the murder of his predecessor.

Known for:

- Being a harsh, oppressive, and power-hungry ruler who utilized the tools of manipulation and intimidation in exercising his authority and control.

- Steadily working to diminish the rights and controls of the upper classes and the Senate.

- Doubling Rome's military power by forcing neighboring towns and cities to cede control of their armies to his authority.

- Engaging in constant construction projects, sometimes destroying the sacred buildings of other tribes.

- Inspiring rebellion and the overthrow and abandonment of the monarchy.

The straw that broke the camel's back, as the saying goes, which inspired rebellion and the subsequent overthrow of Superbus in 509 BCE, was an act of rape. The despicable deed was done by his son to a Roman consul's wife, Lucretia. She shared an account of the experience with her husband and father before killing herself, distraught from shame. This stirred the public's anger and led to an uprising, which sent the king into exile and marked the end of the period of the monarchy.

The Roman Republic (509 – 27 BCE)

Outraged and no longer tolerant to the idea of a one-man rule by a monarch after the oppressive reign of Tarquin the Proud, the senate and people of Rome determined that a new king would not be elected. Instead, the Senate would exercise primary control of the state. The role of the king was divided into two positions serving as heads of state, annually elected magistrates called consuls.

It was thought that having two individuals in equal positions of power would help to prevent one or the other from over-reaching and attempting to exercise excessive control. To further prevent corruption and political decisions that could work against the best interest of Rome as a whole, the Senate determined that consuls would be held legally accountable for their actions. They can face prosecution, even after their annual term, for any misdeed committed during their year in power.

The era of the Republic was marked by a large expansion of territory, pushing Rome's borders further outward. This was facilitated by numerous victories in a long series of wars, which was another notable feature of this era.

There were struggles on the domestic front as well. A major one that the city and Senate contended with during the period of the Republic was the increasing conflict that resulted from deep class divisions within Roman society. The massive divide between the classes sparked a series of civil wars, each driven on both sides by powerful individuals who roused support from the people, to further causes in the effort to address disparities in status and opportunity among the Romans.

A String of Wars

The Roman Republic was engaged in a series of wars and conflicts, both internally and externally. It not only influenced the size and shape of its overall territory but also relationships within the populace and with outside peoples.

Samnite Wars (343 - 282 BCE)

Rome engaged in three wars fought over a 61-year period with the Samnite Kingdom, which was located on the east of Rome. Due to its location, it posed a threat of meaningful proportions to the territories of the Republic.

The First Samnite War is difficult to accurately chronicle because of the engagement of so many parties and the variety of shifting alliances. Even the historians of the day had a difficult time keeping track of specific events and their significance. However, it is generally understood that Rome became involved when it sought to assist people who were living in the nearby highlands, against attacks from the Samnites and other groups.

The Second Samnite War was a power struggle that lasted for 22 years, focused on the control over the city of Naples. It was a long conflict that resulted in heavy losses on both sides; however, Rome eventually dominated and asserted its hold over the central region of the Italian peninsula.

The Third Samnite War involved the collaboration of Gauls, Umbrians, Etruscans, and Samnites, in a bid to defeat Rome. Yet, the Republic was ultimately successful in spite of the impressive alliance formed by its enemies. After this victory, the Roman dominance of central Italy was assured and unchallenged.

Pyrrhic Wars – 280 to 275 BCE

The Pyrrhic wars were fought between Tarentum and Rome. Pyrrhic refers to the king of Epirus in Greece, Pyrrhus. The Tarentum was a Spartan colony located in the Southern Italian coast.

The war started when Roman warships sailed through the bay in Tarentum in order to protect Thurii. This violated a treaty with Tarentum, which forbade the Romans to sail past the Lacinian Promontory of Croton.

Tarentines were not hesitant at all, and they soon sank five of Rome's ten vessels. Rome quickly declared war. As a result, Tarentum contacted Pyrrhus for help.

There were three major battles in the Pyrrhic war:

- Battle of Heraclea in 280 BCE – Pyrrhic victory

- Battle of Asculum in 279 BCE – Pyrrhic victory

- Battle of Beneventum in 275 BCE – Roman victory

In the end, Rome won the war when they laid siege to the city of Tarentum in 272 BCE.

Punic Wars – 264 to 146 BCE

There were three Punic wars that took place between Rome and Carthage. They started in 264 BCE and ended when Carthage was destroyed in 146 BCE. Throughout the Italian peninsula, Rome had become a dominant power before the First Punic War broke out. Carthage, on the other hand, was a powerful city-state located in Northern Africa and was widely known for its maritime strength.

Rome, in 264 BCE, decided to intervene in a dispute between Sicily, a Carthaginian province at that time, and Messina, which involved an attack by Syracuse soldiers against Messina. Carthage sided with Syracuse while Rome sided with Messina. The disagreement eventually exploded in a war that pitted these two powers, with Sicily at stake. Within the 20 years that formed part of the lengthy conflict, Rome rebuilt its fleet so it could confront Carthage's navy. The Roman ships scored their first sea victory at Mylae in 260 BCE, although their invasion of North Africa was not so successful. By the end of the First

Punic War, Rome took over the control of Sicily as its first overseas province.

Before the Second Punic War began, Rome had gained dominance over Sardinia and Corsica. Carthage, though, had managed to create an influence over Spain by 237 BCE, under the leadership of Hamilcar Barca and his then son-in-law, Hasdrubal. Legend says that Barca died in 229 BCE and made his younger son, Hannibal, swear a blood oath against Rome. When Hasdrubal died in 221 BCE, Hannibal took charge of the Carthaginian forces in Spain. In two years, he led his army into Saguntum, an Iberian city under Roman protection. Thus, the Second Punic War began.

Hannibal gained quite a few victories during his march from Spain to Italy. His conquest reached its height at Cannae in 216 BCE when his cavalry surrounded Rome's. Rome rebounded, and the Carthaginians soon lost their hold over Italy after Roman victories in North Africa and Spain. Hannibal's troops had to abandon their fight in Italy so they could defend North Africa. Hannibal's losses put an end to Carthage's empire in the Western Mediterranean. Spain became a territory of Rome and Carthage was left with only its North African territory.

The third war was the most controversial, started by Cato the Elder and other members of the Roman Senate who tried to convince their colleagues that Carthage was still a threat to Rome's supremacy. Technically speaking, Carthage did break their treaty with Rome in 149 BCE, when they declared war against Numidia. After the war began, the Carthaginians held their own for two years, until the Romans put Scipio Aemilianus in charge of their North African campaign. In 146 BCE, Aemilianus pushed his way into the citadel. After seven days of fighting, Carthage finally surrendered. The war obliterated the 700-year-old city, and its 50,000 surviving citizens were sold into slavery.

Servile Wars - 135 to 71 BCE

There were three slave revolts during this period. The first one took place in Sicily and was led by a slave named Eunus who believed that he had supernatural powers. Cleon was his general and they resisted the Roman forces that were sent to control them. They used guerrilla tactics instead of open warfare. It took Rome three years to kill Cleon and capture Eunus.

After 22 years, another revolt arose in Sicily. However, not much is known about this particular war. It took several years to end as well.

The third conflict forming part of the Servile Wars occurred right in the Italian mainland. An escaped Gladiator, Spartacus, led the slave forces. The Roman Senate did not take the revolt seriously until several militias were defeated. After Spartacus was able to fight off two teams of Roman soldiers, thousands of slaves joined him in the mountains, bringing their ranks up to 70,000. Spartacus met his first defeat in Cisalpine Gaul in 72 BCE, where 20,000 of his men were killed. Still, newcomers continued to join him. Nobody really knows what motivated Spartacus to do so; but, instead of escaping over the Alps, he went back to Southern Italy. In the final battle, Rome had upped its forces and Spartacus knew there was no way out. He and many of his soldiers were killed in the last campaign.

The Decline of the Roman Republic

At this point in the Roman Republic, things started to take a darker turn. The government was not working effectively and there was much civil unrest.

Tribune of the Plebeians

After the Roman Republic was established, the Plebeians were burdened with debts. This caused a series of clashes and almost brought the Plebeians to the brink of revolt. Instead, Lucius Sicinius Vellutus convinced them into seceding. The Senate sent in Agrippa Menenius Lanatus to talk to the group. They worked together and created the first tribune of Plebeians.

They became the most important check on the power of the magistrates and Roman Senate. They could preside over the people's assembly, intervene on behalf of the Plebeians in legal issues, propose legislation, and summon the Senate. Their biggest power was the capability to veto the actions of consuls.

Tiberius Gracchus – 133 BCE

Tiberius was a Roman tribune who died in 133 BCE. He sponsored agrarian reforms in order to restore the class of independent farmers. He was assassinated during a riot that was sparked by his opponents in the Senate.

He was born to an aristocratic Roman family. His education in the New Greek enlightenment gave him form and clarity in public speaking. Serving in the Roman military, he came to know about the weakness of Rome. This is what led him to secure a spot on the tribune.

Gaius Gracchus – 122 BCE

Gaius, the brother of Tiberius, was a Roman tribune from 123 to 122 BCE. He worked to reenact the agrarian reform that Tiberius had proposed. After his brother's murder, he joined the outcry against the Scipio Nasica.

While a complete understanding of his tribune career is uncertain because of some ambiguities in chronology, it is clear that he completed his program.

Pompey and Crassus

After Sulla removed the tribune, Pompey and Crassus, in 70 BCE, stood for consul election even though neither of them was legally allowed to do so. Crassus had to wait a year between his praetorship and consulship, and Pompey was too young. Nevertheless, they both ended up winning. They annulled the changes that Sulla made and restored power to the tribune. The Senate did not try to prevent them from doing this because both men had the support of loyal armies.

Julius Caesar

When Caesar took charge, he changed the course of history for the Greco-Roman world in a decisive and irreversible way. The Caesars family belonged to the patrician class, but this did not assure political advantage anymore. On the contrary, it was a handicap because family members were debarred from holding para-constitutional offices. The Caesars were not the snobbish or conservative-minded type of Patricians.

Caesar was born on July 12, 100 BCE. He carried his father's name. Caesar's father governed the province of Asia as praetor. Caesar's mother was Aurelia Cotta, who was also of noble birth. He was raised by parents who held a Populare ideology of Rome. This view favored a democratization of the government and wanted the Plebeians to be given better rights, as opposed to the views of the Optimate faction.

It is important to note that the Populare and the Optimate were not political parties in conflict like the ones we have today. Instead, they were political ideologies which a lot of people shifted towards and from, no matter what their class was in society. The concept of appealing to people who supported him, rather than trying to gain the approval of the members of the Senate or of the other Patricians, would end up helping Caesar later on.

Caesar's father died when he was 16, and he became the head of the family. He believed that being part of the priesthood would help his family the most. He was able to get himself nominated a High Priest of Jupiter. In order to qualify for the position, one had to be a patrician and be married to another patrician. Because of these rules, Caesar had to break off his engagement with a plebeian girl.

In 84 BCE, Caesar married a patrician by the name of Cornelia, the daughter of Lucius Cornelius Cinna. The marriage publicly placed him on the radical side. Once Sulla declared himself as a dictator, he started a purge of his enemies, especially those who held the Populare ideology. Sulla ordered Caesar to divorce his wife but he refused. His defiance caused Caesar to be targeted, and he fled from Rome. His title was stripped and his wife's dowry was taken away.

Caesar left Italy and joined the military service in order to support his family. He proved to be a good soldier and was awarded the civic crown when he saved a life during battle.

After Sulla's death, Caesar returned to Rome and tried his hand at being an orator. He turned out to be an eloquent speaker.

While sailing to Greece in 75 BCE, a group of pirates kidnapped Caesar and held him for ransom. He always had a high opinion of himself, and when he was told that he was being held for 20 talents, Caesar said that he was worth at least fifty. During his captivity, the pirates treated him well and he made sure to stay friendly with them. He repeatedly told the pirates that once he was released, he would find and then crucify them for hurting his family. They thought that he was only joking. However, when he was released, he made good on this threat. He found the pirates and had their throats slit before being crucified.

Working with Pompey, Caesar worked to undo the Sullan constitution. In 65 BCE, Caesar was elected one of the curule aediles. During this time, he lived lavishly on borrowed money. In 63 BCE, he became pontifex maximus through a political dodge. At this point, he had established himself as a controversial political figure.

First Triumvirate

The First Triumvirate was established with the alliance of Crassus, Pompey, and Julius Caesar. The trio dominated the Roman Republic from 60 BCD to 53 BCE. The unstable government and a near civil war caused these three men to set aside their opposing views and join forces, controlling the Roman political world for almost a decade. Julius Caesar eventually rose above all the other two.

The three knew that, together, they could achieve their goals. Caesar first had to reconcile the differences between Crassus and Pompey. In order to seal their alliance, Caesar had his daughter, Julie, marry Pompey.

Once Caesar's consulship ended, he moved his army over the Alps and into Gaul. He returned to Italy in 50 BCE, victorious. Pompey, however, was jealous of his success. He eventually became governor of Spain. Crassus was awarded an army but never realized his goals because he was killed in the Battle of Carrhae in 53 BCE. His death spelled doom for the triumvirate. The death of Caesar's daughter, Julia, split the alliance even further.

Pompey eventually fled to Egypt where the Egyptians had him murdered because they believed the gods favored Caesar. Caesar took off to Egypt to pursue Pompey, and was outraged when he found out that he had been killed. He proclaimed martial law and took over.

Caesar, in secret, sent for Cleopatra VII. She had been exiled and had herself smuggled through enemy lines. He aligned himself with her, starting a war between the Egyptian army and Caesar's legions. They were besieged in the palace by the Egyptians before Roman reinforcements showed up six months later, on March of 47 BCE. They then defeated the Egyptian army.

Cleopatra and Caesar had become lovers during this short meeting, and he stayed with her in Egypt for nine months. In 47 BCE, Cleopatra gave birth to a son, Ptolemy Caesar, who was most commonly known as Caesarion. The boy was named as her successor and heir.

During this time, Pharnaces created a rebellion in the East and Caesar left to crush it, leaving Cleopatra as Egypt's ruler. Caesar's troops marched through Asia Minor and defeated the tribes. He then turned his focus back to the people in Rome. During the Battle of Thapsus, Caesar's troops were able to defeat the forces of the Optimate faction. He returned to Rome, triumphant, in July of 46 BCE.

Cleopatra had hoped that Caesar would legitimize Caesarion as his son and heir. He didn't. Instead, he chose to name Gaius Octavius Thurinus, his grandnephew, as his heir. He did allow Cleopatra and their son, as well as their entourage, to move to a comfortable home in Rome. He visited them frequently even though he was already married to Calpurnia. The Senate was very upset with this, as Rome had strict laws against bigamy. Still, Caesar was designated as Dictator Perpetuus, giving him the title of dictator for life.

He initiated several reforms that included land redistribution for the veterans and the poor, which would eliminate the need for displacement of other citizens. He also devised political reforms that ended up being unpopular with the Senate. He did not rule with the Senate's approval in mind. He typically told them the laws that he wanted to have passed, and how quickly they should be done. All of these were done in the hopes of advancing and consolidating his power.

He changed the calendar, created a police force, and had the Carthage rebuilt. He also got rid of the tax system, among several other pieces of legislation. During the time that he ruled as a dictator, Romans enjoyed prosperous times. However, members of the Senate, especially those leaning towards the Optimate faction, were worried that he would end up becoming too powerful. They feared that he might get rid of the Senate altogether.

In 44 BCE, on March 15th, while at the portico of the basilica of Pompey the Great, Caesar was assassinated by a group of senators. One of the most well-known assassins was Marcus Junius Brutus, Caesar's second choice for his heir. Gaius Cassius Longinus was also an assassin. There were other assassins as well. Some stories say that there may have been as many as sixty.

Caesar ended up being stabbed 23 times before he died on the base of the statue of Pompey. The problem for the assassins was that they never made a plan on what to do after they killed Caesar. By neglecting this part of their mission, they did not get rid of Marcus Antonius, Caesar's cousin, and right-hand man. Mark Antony turned the tables on the killers, partnering with Octavian and using Rome's popular opinion against the perpetrators.

Second Triumvirate

After the murder of Julius Caesar in 44 BCE, Octavian, Mark Antony, and Lepidus formed the Second Triumvirate. The three men vowed that they would get revenge on the killers and would stabilize the Roman Republic, in what ended up being its death throes.

The assassins of Caesar had believed that by killing him, they would bring back the faith and spirit that the Roman people used to have in the Republic. Without an exit strategy, Brutus fled to the Theater of Pompey. The Senate had gathered at the Temple of Jupiter on Capitoline Hill to address the citizens. They had expected a warm reception but this was not the case. The people were hostile towards them and did not like the Senate's pleas for amnesty and compromise. The assassins had to flee the city, with Cassius and Brutus making their way to the East.

The new triumvirate was, at best, unstable. Mark Antony and Octavian distrusted each other. Each of them believed that he was the rightful heir to lead the government. Antony added fuel to the fire when he blocked Octavian from gaining access to his stepfather's money. Lepidus, who was the most ineffective of the three, was named the Chief Priest. Antony appointed him even though the title was supposed to have been given to Octavian.

Antony was viewed by the Senate as an even more dangerous tyrant. He tried to take control over the government after Caesar's death and brought about the ire of the Senate. All of this ended up causing its members to declare Antony an enemy. Eventually, Lepidus was also declared an enemy after he voiced out his support of Antony. Antony managed to anger a number of important Roman citizens. Marcus Tullius Cicero, who was a Roman poet and statesman, wrote several scathing essays stating his distaste of Antony. Cicero once said:
"Now listen, I beg you, Senators, I do not mean to the personal and domestic scandals created by Antony's disgusting improprieties, but to the evil, godless way in which he has undermined us all, and our fortunes, and our whole country."

The desire to avenge the death of Caesar brought the three together. With a long list of enemies, they turned to Sextus Pompey, Cassius, and Brutus. Antony battled Cassius and Brutus at Philippi. Cassius had Brutus decapitate him so that he would not be captured. Brutus was able to escape but ended up committing suicide.

Even though Octavian was only 19 years old, he garnered the support of the majority of the Roman army, especially from those who had been loyal followers of Caesar. Octavian, in 43 BCE, demanded that the Senate provide him with political authority, which he needed. This meant a consulship. The Senate, however, refused to grant his demand since he was not even close to the age requirement of 33 years. His soldiers marched into the Senate with their swords drawn. The Senate quickly reversed its decision and provided him with a consulship as well as a co-consul, Quintus Pedius. They enacted Lex Pedia, which undid the prior ruling that had given all the conspirators immunity. The decree created a new law that condemned all of the people involved in the murder of Caesar. This included Sextus Pompey who was not even part of the actual murder.

Despite their victories, the days of the triumvirate were numbered. While Lepidus had helped with Pompey, his continued failures in battle led to Octavian banishing him to Circei. The empire was then divided between Antony and Octavian. Antony would meet Cleopatra VII of Egypt. Their love would eventually lead to war.

Antony and Cleopatra planned to trap Octavian at his fleet in Actium. Their plan was flawed from the beginning, and most of the members of Antony's team did not favor a woman having political say. Even though they outnumbered Octavian's troops, they failed. The lovers narrowly escaped; Cleopatra to Egypt and Antony to Libya. When their plans to raise more troops proved unsuccessful, the only option for Antony was suicide. Cleopatra tried her best to reach a compromise with Octavian. When this strategy failed, Cleopatra took her own life as well.
When Octavian returned to Rome, the Roman Republic was finished. Thus began the Roman Empire. He was quickly named the first emperor of Rome, Augustus. Augustus set the stage for everybody who would follow him.

Chapter 2: The Era of Empire

After the Battle of Actium, Gaius Octavian Thurinus, the heir of Caesar, was crowned the first Roman emperor. When he took over the throne, he was named Augustus Caesar. The Senate willingly gave Augustus the title of emperor. They lavished him with power and praise because he destroyed their enemies and brought stability.

Augustus ruled as emperor of Rome from 31 BCE until his death in 14 CE. During this time, he declared that he "found Rome a city of clay but left it a city of marble." Augustus was able to reform laws and secured Rome's borders. He also initiated a large number of building projects, which was mostly performed by his right-hand man, Agrippa. The first Pantheon was among these. Through all of his work, he ended up securing the name of the greatest cultural and political powers in history. He initiated what they called the Pax Romana. This was a time of prosperity and peace, which was unknown until that time and lasted over 200 years.

After Augustus died, power was passed on to Tiberius. He continued the former emperor's policies, but he lacked the vision and strength of character that defined his predecessor. This same issue continued with the three succeeding emperors: Caligula, Claudius, and Nero. These five emperors of the Roman Empire came to be known as the Julio-Claudian Dynasty.

Caligula is commonly known for his insanity and depravity; though early on in his rule, he was actually quite commendable. This is also true for Claudius, his successor. Claudius was able to grow Rome's territory and power in Britain. Caligula and Claudius were assassinated while in office. The Praetorian Guard of Caligula murdered him, but for Claudius, it was his wife who committed the deed. Nero's suicide brought an end to the Julio-Claudian Dynasty. This caused a period of unrest among the Romans and became known as The Year of Four Emperors.

The Year of Four Emperors

The emperors that made up this period were Galba, Otho, Vitellius, and Vespasian. In 68 CE, after Nero committed suicide, Galba took over the role of emperor. He instantly proved that he was unfit for the responsibility. He, too, ended up being assassinated by the Praetorian Guard. Otho succeeded him on the very day he died. Initially, it was believed that he would make a good emperor. Unfortunately, the Romans were not able to find out. General Vitellius wanted to be in power; thus, he created a small civil war that ended in Otho committing suicide. This gave Vitellius the chance to take the throne.

He proved that he was just as unfit as Galba had been. He started engaging in luxurious feasts and entertainment instead of doing what an emperor was supposed to do. Vespasian's legions then declared that he should become emperor. Vespasian's men murdered Vitellius, and he took the throne exactly a year after Galba had ascended it.

During his rule, Vespasian created the Flavian Dynasty which was made up of empire expansion, economic prosperity, and massive building projects. Vespasian remained emperor from 69 to 79 CE. He started the construction of the Flavian Amphitheatre, which is now known as the Colosseum of Rome. Titus, his son, took over after his father's death and completed the building of the Colosseum. He ruled from 79 to 81 CE.

During Titus' reign, Rome saw the eruption of Mount Vesuvius in 79 CE. The catastrophe buried the cities of Herculaneum and Pompeii.

Titus died in 81 CE from a fever. His brother, Domitian, then took over and ruled from 81 to 96 CE. He secured and expanded the Roman boundaries, and repaired the damage that had been caused by the fire. He continued the building projects began by his brother and he was also able to improve the empire's economy. Even though all of this, his autocratic policies and methods caused the Senate to dislike him. In 96 CE, Domitian was assassinated.

Five Good Emperors

Nerva took over after Domitian's assassination. Nerva created the Nervan-Antonine Dynasty, which ruled Rome from 96 to 192 CE. This period was marked by prosperity due to the five good emperors, bringing the Roman Empire to greater heights:
1. Nerva – 96 to 98 CE

2. Trajan – 98 to 117 CE

3. Hadrian – 117 to 138 CE

4. Antoninus Pius – 138 to 161 CE

5. Marcus Aurelius – 161 to 180 CE

The Roman Empire became stronger, more stable, and expanded further under their rule. Commodus and Lucius Verus were the last rulers of the Nervan-Antonine Dynasty. Verus was co-emperor under the rule of Marcus Aurelius until he died in 169 CE. It seems as though he was ineffective.

The successor and son of Aurelius, Commodus, was the biggest disgrace of all the emperors of Rome. He has depicted the world over as one who indulged his whims at the expense of Rome. He ended up being strangled in his bath by his own wrestling partner, in 192 CE. This ended the Dynasty and brought Pertinax to power.

The Severan Dynasty

For three months, Pertinax was Rome's ruler before he was assassinated. The Year of the Five Emperors then began and concluded in Septimus Severus' rise to power. He was the ruler of Rome from 193 to 211 CE. During his reign, he was able to defeat the Parthians and enlarged the size of the empire. All of his campaigns in Britain and Africa were costly and extensive. This was likely the cause of Rome's financial struggles. His successors were his sons Geta and Caracalla. Caracalla eventually had his brother killed and stayed as ruler until 217 CE, when his bodyguard killed him.

During his reign, Roman citizenship was extended to all free men in the empire. It is believed that the law was created to raise tax revenues. The Severan Dynasty continued until Alexander Severus was assassinated in 235 CE. This caused the Roman Empire to plunge into what is known as The Crisis of the Third Century.

Two Empires

The time labeled as The Imperial Crisis in Roman history was marked by a never-ending civil war, as different leaders tried to gain control over the Roman Empire. There was widespread economic instability, social unrest, and the breaking up of the empire into three regions. It was Aurelian who reunited it. His policies were improved and developed upon by Diocletian who created the Tetrarchy in order to keep the empire in order.

To make the administration of such a vast empire more efficient, Diocletian halved it in 285 CE. This act created the Western and the Eastern Empires. The Eastern section is commonly referred to as the Byzantine Empire. Since the past crisis arose due to problems with succession, Diocletian declared that all future successors needed to be picked and approved at the beginning of one's rule. His two identified successors were Constantine and Maxentius. However, he did away with the rule in 305 CE, causing the tetrarchy to dissolve as the empire's regions fought for dominance. After Diocletian died in 311 CE, Constantine and Maxentius led the empire into another civil war.

Chapter 3: The Christianization, Splitting, and Fall of the Empire

Constantine was able to defeat Maxentius in 312 CE at the Battle of the Milvian Bridge. He took over as the emperor of both regions and ruled from 306 to 337 CE. Constantine strongly believed Jesus had been the reason why he won. Because of this belief, Constantine started a series of laws that specified a tolerance for the religion that became known as Christianity.

Like many other Roman emperors who believed they had a connection with some deity that improved their standing and authority, Constantine's chosen figure was Jesus Christ. In 325 CE, he presided over the First Council of Nicea to create rules for the faith. They worked to name the divinity of Jesus and how they should create the manuscript that is now known as *The Bible*. He was able to stabilize the empire, reform the military, and revalue the currency. He also managed to found the city named New Rome. It was where the former city of Byzantium stood, which eventually became known as Constantinople. It is now modern-day Istanbul.

Many Christians who saw him as a champion of their faith named him Constantine the Great. But for several historians, the honor could have also been due to his political, religious, and cultural reforms, as well as his battle skills. After he died, his sons took over the empire. They soon got involved in various conflicts, which would threaten everything that Constantine had accomplished.

Constantine's three sons, named Constans, Constantius II, and Constantine II, split the empire into thirds; but they were soon fighting over who should have more. During these conflicts, Constans and Constantine II were killed. The third brother died after he named his cousin, Julian, as his heir. Julian took over as ruler for only two years. He tried to return Rome to what it used to be through different reforms that were supposed to improve the government's efficiency.

Since Julian was a Neo-Platonic philosopher, he rejected Christian views and blamed Constantine's beliefs for the empire's decline. While he claimed to have religious tolerance, Julian got rid of all Christians in government positions, barred Christians from serving in the military, and banned the teaching of their religion. He died during his campaign against the Persians, officially ending Constantine's dynasty. He was the last pagan emperor to rule Rome. Because of his opposition to Christianity, he became known as "Julian the Apostate."
Jovian briefly ruled Rome and brought Christianity back as the main faith. He abolished several edicts Julian had established. After his death, Theodosius I became emperor. He carried on Jovian's and Constantine's religious reforms, outlawing pagan worship in the empire, converting pagan temples to Christian churches, and closing universities and schools.

Notably, he closed Plato's Academy. A lot of his reforms were unpopular among the common people and the Roman aristocracy who still held traditional pagan practices. The unified religious beliefs and social duties were impeded by a religion that got rid of other deities, proclaiming instead that there was a single God that ruled from the heavens. Since Theodosius I was such a devout Christian, he neglected all his other duties as emperor. He ended up being the last emperor to rule the Western and Eastern Empires.

The Fall of the Empire

During 376 to 382 CE, Rome was caught up in several battles against the Goths. These became known as the Gothic Wars. On August 9, 378 CE, at the Battle of Adrianople, the Roman Emperor Valens was defeated. This is marked by historians as a pivotal point in the fall of the West.

Orosius argued that Christianity did not play a role in the fall of Rome. He believed that pagan practices were to blame instead. Some of the other influences that people believe contributed to the fall of the empire include government corruption, the large size of land, and the increasing strength of Germanic tribes. The Roman military was no longer able to keep the borders safe as they once had, nor was the government able to collect the taxes. The arrival of the Visigoths in the third century, along with the ensuing instances of rebellion, were all contributing factors to the decline of Rome.

On September 4, 476 CE, the Western Roman Empire officially ended when Romulus Augustus was killed by the German king, Odoacer. The Eastern Empire survived a while longer under the Byzantine Empire, lasting until 1453 CE. What remained no longer resembled the original empire. The Western Empire was re-invented as The Holy Roman Empire, but was a far cry from the original Roman Empire. The only similarity was in the name.

Legacy

The innovations and inventions created by the empire altered the lives of the citizens, and are still being used in many cultures around the world. Advancements in construction such as fast-drying cement, aqueducts, indoor plumbing, buildings, and roads were either created or improved by the Romans. The Western calendar came from the one that Caesar had created, and all the names of the months and days of the week are Roman in origin

Socks, newspapers, keys, locks, public toilets, and apartment complexes were created by Rome's inhabitants; as well as satire literature, magnifying glasses, cosmetics, the postal system, and shoes. During the empire's height, there were large developmental advances in warfare, government, religion, law, and medicine. Romans were adept in borrowing things and improving on them. This makes it hard to figure out what was really theirs and what was not. What we do know for sure is that they did leave an enduring legacy which still influences people today.

Chapter 4: Plebeians and Patricians

In ancient Rome, the citizens were divided between two classes: the Patricians and the Plebeians. The wealthy members of the upper class were the Patricians. The rest were referred to as Plebeians.

Patricians

The Patricians were the ruling class of the Roman Empire. There were only certain families that could be part of this class. All Patricians had to be born into the title. Though they made up a small portion of the total population of Rome, they held all the power.

Patricians were the true descendants of the original natives of Rome. Still, the origin of the class remains obscure. The issue as to when the exclusive caste was decided upon and clearly defined remains uncertain. It is believed, though, that this was through the efforts of King Servius Tullius, when he required people to register. The registration and division of citizens according to tribes and wealth created distinction between the two classes.

With the development of the Assembly of the Centuries from a military to a political group, a way was provided for wealthier Plebeians to have an influential vote in legislation and elections. The expulsion of the kings, who might have been able to check patrician control, gave the ruling class an opportunity to retain possession of religious and legal knowledge, priesthoods, and magistracies to themselves.

The struggle of the Roman Republic stemmed from the continued efforts of the Plebeians to achieve political equality, to break up the religious and political monopoly set in place by the Patricians, and to secure economic relief for the poorer people.

Even though they did have a lot more power than the Plebeians, Patricians had to be careful. The Plebeians made up the majority of the population, so they could turn dangerous if angered. In order to avoid conflict, they were always faced with giving the Plebeians with just enough rights to appease them. They did their best to retain most of the power.

Towards the end of the Roman Republic, Patricians kept exclusive control only to a few positions in the priesthood, Senate leaders, and the interim head of state. During the late republic, the differences between the two classes started to lose their political importance.

Once Rome reached the empire period, having a patrician rank was a requirement for someone to ascend the throne. Only the emperor was able to create new Patricians. In order for the ancient priesthood to continue, Patricians did not have many privileges other than fewer military obligations. After the reign of Constantine ended, *Patricius* became a more personal title instead of a hereditary one of honor. It ranked third after the emperor and consuls but did not provide any sort of power.

Their responsibilities included:
- Care for and the supervision of the land.

- If they were part of the Senate, they had the responsibilities of the Senate.

Their rights included:
- Creating laws that would go to the assembly.

- Being the only people who were allowed to become senators.

- Having economic and political advantages.

Plebeians

Anybody that was not a patrician was known as a plebeian. Plebeians consisted of soldiers, laborers, craftsmen, and farmers.

Plebeians were sometimes referred to as Plebian. The distinction between the two classes was probably based on the influence and wealth of certain families who started the patrician clan under the very early republic during the fifth and fourth centuries BCE.

Originally, Plebeians were not allowed to join the Senate or any other public office except for the military tribune. Before the 445 BCE passage of the Lex Canuleia law, they could only marry other Plebeians.

Their responsibilities included:
- Fighting in the Roman army.

- Working for the Patricians' land.

Unfortunately, Plebeians did not have any rights because they were merely seen as "common folk." Eventually, though, they fought and were given the right to participate in politics.

Early Rome

There were a lot of differences between the Plebeians and Patricians. These included responsibilities and rights, power levels, and population levels, among other things. Patricians wanted to make sure that they retained the majority of the power, but they needed to have the Plebeians on their side to do it.

The Plebeians had very little rights during the early stages of Rome. Every single religious and government position was held by a patrician. They were the ones who created the laws, owned all of the lands, and held the position of general in the army. Plebeians were not allowed to hold any sort of public office and they could not even marry Patricians.

Since the Plebeians worked as foot soldiers, they fought most of the Roman battles and helped in Rome's expansion. This meant that they expanded the influence that the Patricians had. Patricians were often resented for the power they held, but the Patricians likely feared the Plebeians because they made up a large portion of the population.

Since being plebeian or patrician was based on family relations, no intermarriage was allowed during the early days of Rome. In order to make sure that the Plebeians continued to fight their wars, they later changed this law.

Plebeian Revolt

At around 494 BCE, the Plebeians started to fight against the rules established by the Patricians. This was known as the "Conflict of the Orders." During the course of around 200 years, the Plebeians made attempts to obtain more rights. They went on strike in order to protest. They left the city for a long while, refusing to work or fight in the army. Eventually, through several revolts, the Plebeians they were able to gain a number of rights, which included being allowed to run for office and to marry Patricians.

Their campaign lasted until 287 BCE. The Plebeians organized themselves into different corporations and withdrew from the state during at least five critical occasions in order to compel the Patricians to concede. One such time was when their withdrawal was called secession.

The plebeian group held their own assemblies and elected their own officials. These tribunes were normally Plebeians who were more well-to-do than the others. The most important step in the campaign of the Plebeians was achieving the inviolability of their tribunes. The campaign ended when Quintus Hortensius, a plebeian dictator, was appointed. He created the law, Lex Hortensia, which made approved measures in their assembly binding; not only to the Plebeians but to the entire community. Later in the Republic and in the Empire as well, the term was still used to describe any of the commoners.

The Law of Twelve Tables

One of the first concessions that the Plebeians saw after their revolt was the Law of the Twelve Tables. These laws were displayed in public where everybody could see them. They were put in place to protect most of the basic rights of Roman citizens, no matter what their social class was.

The Twelve Tables were supposed to have been written by ten commissioners, at the insistence of the Plebeians. They felt that their legal rights had been hampered by the fact that the judgments were based on unwritten customs preserved by a very small group of Patricians.

They started in 451, and the first set of commissioners created ten tables. These were then supplemented with two additional tables later on. All were formally posted in 450. They were likely written on bronze tablets and placed in the Roman Forum. This written code allowed the Plebeians to become more acquainted with the law, helping to protect them against any abuse of power on the Patricians' part.

These Twelve Tables were not a liberalizing of a certain custom or a reform. Instead, they recognized the feelings of the patrician class and the patriarchal family, the interference of religion in civil cases, and the validity of enslavement for debts that had not been paid.
The fact that they show a remarkable amount of liberality for their time when it comes to testamentary rights and contract, has probably less to do with the innovations of decemvirs, and more to do with the progress that had been made in commercial customs during a time of vigorous trade and prosperity.

Since there are only a few random quotations from the Twelve Tables that are extant today, knowledge about what they actually contained largely comes from the reference in later juridical writings. While they were held in high honor by Romans as the prime legal source, they were superseded through later changes in the law but were never actually abolished.

The following are what we know about what the twelve tables covered:

- Table 1 – procedure for trials and courts.

- Table 2 – continuation for trails and theft.

- Table 3 – how debt is handled.

- Table 4 – the rights of the fathers over their family.

- Table 5 – the legal inheritance and guardianship laws.

- Table 6 – acquisition and possession.

- Table 7 – land rights and crimes.

- Table 8 – torts and delicts.

- Table 9 – the public law.

- Table 10 – the sacred law.

- Table 11 – supplemental information one.

- Table 12 – supplemental information two.

Plebeian Officers

Eventually, Plebeians got to elect their own officials in the government. These people were known as tribunes who represented the other Plebeians and who fought for their kind's rights. They were able to veto new laws that the Roman Senate created.

Plebeian Nobles

As time passed, there were fewer legal differences between the Patricians and Plebeians. The Plebeians were able to be elected to the Senate and they were even allowed to hold the title of consul. Furthermore, Plebeians were allowed to get married to Patricians. Wealthy Plebeians even ended up becoming part of the Roman nobility. However, even though there were a lot of changes in their laws, the Patricians always had most of the power and wealth in Ancient Rome.

Chapter 5: A Melting Pot of Theism

In most societies, whether they are modern or ancient, religion has played a major role during their development. In the beginning, the religion of Rome was polytheistic. Rome had an array of spirits and gods, and more were added to include foreign cults and Greek gods. When the empire began to expand, Romans did not impose their beliefs on the people they conquered. This should not be thought of as tolerance, as proven in the way that they responded to the Christian and Jewish population. Christianity would eventually replace all of these gods.

Early Influences and Beliefs

The earliest form of religion in Rome was animistic. They believed spirits inhabited everything, including people. The citizens thought they were watched by their ancestors' spirits. In the beginning, a Capitoline Triad was added to the spirits. These new gods were Mars, Quirinus, and Jupiter. Mars was the god of war and thought to be the father of Remus and Romulus, the founders of Rome. Quirinus was Romulus after he had been deified. He watched over all the inhabitants of Rome. Jupiter was a supreme god. These three, as well as several others, were worshipped at Capitoline Hill. Because of the Etruscans, this triad will change and include Jupiter as the supreme god; Minerva, who was Jupiter's daughter; and Juno, who was his sister and wife.

Through the influence of Greek colonies found across the Lower Peninsula, many of the gods worshiped in Greece were taken in by the Romans. Myth and religion were one. Roman gods were more anthropomorphic because of the Greek influence. They now had human characteristics of hate, love, jealousy, etc. Romans believed that individual expression was not important, but strict adherence to rituals was. By doing this, they avoided the problems of religious zeal. Each city would come up with its own set of deities and would perform its own religious rites. They built temples throughout the empire to honor their gods. These temples were the god's home and worship was done outside of the temple. Even though the fusion of Greek and Roman deities did influence Rome in a lot of ways, their religion stayed very practical.

They had four separate colleges for priests, although they did not have a priestly class. It was a public office, not a holy one. This practice extended all the way to the imperial palace.

Emperor Augustus took the title of chief priest. Besides the chief priest, some individuals had the ability to read a bird's flight. Others could read the entrails of animals in order to find out the will of the gods, or interpret omens. They would perform elaborate rituals in order to bring victory to Rome during battle. They never went into war or declared war without approval from the gods. From Etruscans times, a diviner was always consulted. They believed that it was very bad to ignore omens. A Roman soothsayer, Spurinna, saw Julius Ceasar's death on the Ides of March upon reading animal entrails. One Roman Commander, Publius Claudius Pulcher, ignored omens and did not eat the sacred chicken before battle during the First Punic War. He was defeated and his military career ended.

The Pantheon

When studying Roman mythology, the emphasis is put on major gods like Juno, Pluto, Neptune, and Jupiter. There were also many minor goddesses and gods like Pax, Cupid, Nemesis, and the Furies.

When you look at Roman religion, you have to look at the impact from the important gods. Foremost are Jupiter and his sister/wife Juno. Jupiter was the sky god, the king of the gods. He controlled the weather and the forces of nature, using thunderbolts to warn the Romans. He was originally the farming god but his role began changing as the city's size got larger. He eventually had his own temple at Capitoline Hill. His supremacy was temporarily set aside while during the reign of Emperor Elagabalus, who replaced Rome's top deity with the Syrian god, Elagabal. Once the emperor was assassinated, Alexander Severus returned Jupiter to his rightful place. Juno came next. She was Jupiter's sister/wife. The month June is named after her. She is a supreme goddess who has her own temple on Esquiline Hill. She is believed to be the goddess of the moon and light. She shows all of the virtues of matronhood. As the goddess of fertility and childbirth, she is Juno Lucina.

Next, come Minerva, and Mars, the war god. Legend states that Minerva sprang out of Jupiter's head. A goddess of education, industry, and commerce, she would later on be regarded as the goddess of war, craftsmen, musicians, and doctors. Mars has a temple that was dedicated by Emperor Augustus to honor the death of the assassins of Julius Caesar. Sacrifices would be made to him before and after battles by Roman commanders. The day of the week, Tuesday, was named after him.

Cult Worship

Other than worshipping the above gods, the Romans worshiped many cults such as the Imperial Cult, Sibyl, Sarapis, Isis, Cybele, and Bacchus. Some of these were accepted by society while others brought fear. Bacchus was a wine god. He is the main reason for the festivals that took place on March 17th. On this day, a young Roman would become a man. As this continued, the Senate soon realized how dangerous this could be, and abolished it in 186 BCE. This only sent the group underground.

Cybele was worshipped by another cult. She was a fertility goddess who has her own temple on Palatine Hill. She is responsible for the well-being of the people. She arrived in Athens in the 5th century BCE, and showed up in Rome in the middle of the Punic Wars. The eunuchs were her priests. Majority of her followers castrated themselves.

Isis is an ancient goddess from Egypt. You might remember her from Egyptian mythology as the mother of Horus and wife of Osiris. Once she became Hellenized, she was the protector of fishermen and sailors.

Sarapis came to Rome from Alexandria. She is the healing god. Sick people would travel miles to be cured at her temple. Sibyl was a priestess of Apollo and traveled from the colony of Cumae in Greece, to Rome. She offered the nine Sibylline Books to the Etruscan King Tarquin. These books are full of prophecies but the king refused because her price was too high. After six of the books were burned, the King reconsidered and decided to buy the remaining three. The Senate consulted these books during emergencies. Unfortunately, they were lost during the barbarian invasion in the fifth century CE.

The thought of deifying an emperor came to life during Emperor Augustus' reign. He would not let the Senate name him a god because he thought he was the son of a god. When he died, the Senate gave him the deification. This was bestowed on many of his successors but some were not bestowed with such distinction. These were Domitian, Nero, Caligula, and Tiberius. They were considered too disgusting to be given such an honor. Nero and Caligula thought they were living gods, and Domitian thought he was the reincarnated Hercules.

Religion Challenged

Christianity and Judaism both posed threats to Rome. They had something in common, as these beliefs refused to worship the Roman gods or make sacrifices to them. Even though the Jews had a firm establishment in the Empire, they were always the target of emperors and were often blamed for everything bad that happened within the empire. Nero even went so far as to banish them out of Rome. Titus continued the war against them during the Jewish Wars. They eventually destroyed Jerusalem and killed thousands.

Christianity was first considered as a sect of Judaism. Nero became suspicious when the Christian group began growing in number. The Great Fire was blamed on the Christians. In retaliation, they called Nero the anti-Christ. In time, Christianity would spread throughout Rome. It appealed to the slaves, women, the illiterate, and the intellectuals. Persecutions got worse and Christian churches were burned. All these continued while Diocletian reigned, ending with the Great Persecution. The Romans thought that Christians offended the "peace of the gods."

Under the reign of Constantine, Christianity received recognition from the Edict of Milan during 313 CE. His compassion toward Christians goes back to the Battle of Milvan Bridge. He believed he saw a cross form in the sky. He thought this vision caused him to be victorious in battle and to become the emperor of Rome. He held a Council of Nicaea in 325 CE, reconciling the differences between the many Christian sects. Under him, churches that had been destroyed were rebuilt. Some people say that he became a Christian on his deathbed.

Christianity would eventually grow and replace all of the traditional religions of Rome. This would make Rome the new Christian center. Yet, Christianity would still take the blame for the misfortunes that happened in the empire. Many people blame the fall of the empire on Christianity. Edward Gibbon thought Christianity absorbed the people's energy and made them unable to handle the problems that were plaguing the empire. In spite of all its lows and highs, beginning from the days of inhabiting spirits to all the gods and goddesses, emperor deification, and on to Christianity, religion has always been an important part of the Roman Empire.

Chapter 6: The Masterpiece That Was Rome

Roman art suffered a crisis to their reputation since it was discovered that the majority actually came from ancient Greece during the 1600s CE and onwards. Once art critics realized that most of the finest pieces were merely copies of some lost Greek originals, they did not appreciate it as much. Roman art had flourished with everything Roman during the Renaissance and medieval times but soon diminished. There were other problems with Roman art such as not really identifying what it actually was. It differed from Greek art, and geography played a big role. It was more diverse as it changed according to location. Even though Rome remained the main focal point, there were other centers that produced art in accordance with the respective tastes and trends of a locality. The most notable are Athens, Antioch, and Alexandria. Because of this, many critics argue that Roman art does not actually exist.

Nowadays, there is a more balanced view of Roman art. Successes in archaeology have caused Roman art to be reviewed, and its contribution to the western world has been made clearer. People hold the opinion that Classical Greek art was the pinnacle of artistic endeavors. Many think that Romans simply fused Etruscan and the best of Greek art. They admit that Roman art is very eclectic, inheriting traits from the Hellenistic world that was forged by Alexander the Great and all his conquests. Since this empire covers a very large and diverse culture, the way in which people appreciated the past and depicted vivid ideas to commemorate persons and events are expressed in various art forms. Coins, epigraphy, monumental architecture, statues, frescoes, pottery, mosaics, glassware, jewelry, and seal-cutting were all created to make

Rome more beautiful. It also conveyed various meanings in fashion and the military.

Works of art were taken from conquered cities and brought to Rome for the citizens to appreciate them. Artists from other countries were employed by the Romans, and they opened schools. They established technical development centers and workshops all over the place. The demand for artwork increased, giving rise to mass production. Objects soon flooded the entire empire. The number of artwork that has survived over the years is mind-blowing. Consider Pompeii. It shows a rare insight into the way that works of art were used to enrich the citizens' lives. It became more personalized and individuals owned many pieces. This can be seen in the creation of lifelike portraits of private citizens, through sculptures and paintings. Unlike other civilizations, art was accessible to the lower classes, not just the wealthy.

Roman Sculpture

These sculptures were blended from the idealized perfection of Classical Greek sculptures, with a greater enthusiasm for realism mixed in. Romans sculptors have preserved invaluable works of art that may have been lost.

By the middle of the first century CE, artists in Rome were trying to create and capture the optical effects of shade and light to create more realism. This type of art was developed from keeping wax funeral masks of dead family members. These were then transferred into stone, producing private busts that would show the subject as flabby, scarred, wrinkled, or old. These busts tell the truth. During the antiquity period, there was a strong move toward impressionism that used abstract forms and tricks of light.

Sculptures also became massive and monumental, with larger-than-life statues of heroes, gods, and emperors. This style is much like the bronze statue of Marcus Aurelius sitting on top of the horse that is in the Capitoline Museum, Rome. Towards the end of the Empire, sculptures began to lack proportion. The heads were often large and figures were flatter, often displaying an influence from Eastern art.

The sculpture on altars and buildings could either be for political purposes or just decorative. Some arches captured in great detail special events showing a certain emperor being victorious. It gave the world a message that this emperor was not to be messed with.

Roman Wall Paintings

The insides of the Roman building were decorated with bold designs. Stucco was utilized to create relief effects. In the first century BCE, military structures, tombs, temples, private homes, and public buildings all across made use of fresco and wall paintings. Designs ranged from impressionistic renderings to realistic details that would cover the ceiling and every available inch of space.

Painters used natural earth tones like dark browns, yellows, and reds. Black and blue were employed for plainer designs. The usual subjects depicted in paintings include architecture, mythological scenes, portraits, fauna, flora, entire gardens, landscapes, and townscapes creating 360-degree panoramas that transport the viewer from a small room to the wide world of the artist's imagination.

Roman Mosaics

These pieces were common in many homes and public places across the empire, from Antioch to Africa. Mosaics were created with small colored squares of shells, stone, pottery, glass, tile, or marble. Each piece measured around .5 and 1.5 cm. but contained fine details. Designs would have a large spectrum of colors and used colored grout to match.

The most popular subjects were scenes of fauna, flora, food, hunting, agriculture, sports, gladiator contests, and mythology. They would even create realistic portraits of Romans. The most famous is from the House of the Faun, Pompeii, showing Alexander the Great on the back of Bucephalus doing battle with Darius III, who is in his war chariot.

Architectural Orders

Architects followed the guidelines that were established by the Classical Greeks like Corinthian, Ionic, and Doric. The Romans, though, favored the Corinthian style in their buildings. They did add their own versions and ideas to the Corinthian capital and became more decorative. There is also a mixture of the volute of the Ionic order and the acanthus leaves of the Corinthian. The Tuscan column was also adapted, which was formed from a Doric column but had a smaller capital, a molded base, and a slender shaft without flutes. This column was used in domestic homes like verandahs and peristyles. Monolithic columns were favored instead of the stacking of many drums on top of each other.

As the Empire continued to expand, craftsmen and ideas became integrated into the architectural industry, many using familiar materials such as marble. The eastern influence is seen in features like ornamental fountains, street colonnades, sculptured pedestals, and papyrus leaves in capitals.

Techniques and Materials

The Temple of Jupiter Stator in Rome was the first building to be made entirely of marble. Marble was not widely used until the Empire period. The marble that came from foreign countries were reserved mainly for columns and imperial projects.

Travertine white limestone was preferred for carvings and could hold up heavy loads. It was a favorite substitute for marble and was mainly utilized for steps, window and door frames, as well as paving.

Architects

Buildings were credited to the persons who conceived the projects and paid for them instead of the architects overseeing their construction. Because of this, architects often remained anonymous. Usually, only architects who were employed by the emperor were well-known. Trajan had a favored architect, Apollodorus of Damascus. His skills were building bridges but he is also recognized for building the Trajan's Forum and Baths in Rome. Celer and Severus were responsible for the magnificent sounding roof on Nero's Golden House.

The most famous architect is Vitruvius. He constructed a basilica in Fano and worked for Augustus and Julius Ceasar. He wrote *On Architecture,* a ten-volume study about the subject. The set of books has survived, completely intact, all these years. It covers all facets of architecture, including advice for people who want to be architects, types of buildings, and a lot more. A quote from Vitruvius sums it up: "All buildings must be executed in such a way as to take account of durability, utility, and beauty."

Key Buildings

Bridges and Aqueducts:

These were massive structures that could have single, double, or triple tiers of arches. They were designed to carry fresh water from sources many miles away.

Basilicas:

These buildings were adopted by the Christian church but were originally built as places for large gatherings, commonly being courts of law. The structure was usually constructed beside the city's marketplace. It was enclosed by colonnades on every side. The basilica's roof and the long hall were likewise supported by piers and columns. The columns form a central nave flanked on every side by an aisle. A gallery runs all around the first floor and an altar is found at either one or both ends. A good example is the Severan Basilica that is located at Lepcis Magna.

Baths:

Roman baths show how well the Romans were at creating breathtaking interior spaces using buttresses, vaults, domes, and arches. The largest was built symmetrically on a single axis and included underfloor heating, libraries, fountains, hot and cold rooms, pools, and inner-wall heating with terracotta piping. The exteriors were normally plain, but the interiors were full of mosaics, statues, marble, and columns. The best surviving example is the Baths of Caracalla located in Rome.

Private Homes:

All of these are famous for their sumptuously decorated interiors through the use of stucco and fresco. These residences might also have fountains, gardens, peristyles, and atriums, all fitting harmoniously together. A good example is the House of the Vettii at Pompeii.

Temples:

Roman temples were a combination of the Greek and Etruscan models. They had an inner chamber at the back of the building that was surrounded by columns and was built on a platform that had a stepped entrance with a columned porch. The columned porch was the focal point of the building. The Maison Carree at Nimes is a complete example. Most temples were rectangular but could also take the shape of a polygon or a circle. The temple of Venus at Baalbeck is a polygonal one.

Amphitheater and Theaters:

Roman theatres are, of course, inspired by the Greeks. The main difference was the orchestra pit that was built in a semi-circular shape, with the entire theatre made from stone. Romans added in a decorated stage building that had many different statues, pediments, projections, and levels of columns. The theatre at Orange is a good example.

The completely enclosed amphitheater was a Roman's favorite. The Colosseum is the most famous and also the largest. It has a highly decorative exterior and the seats are set over many barrel vaults. Underground rooms are situated below the floor of the arena, hiding props, animals and people until they were needed.

Triumphal Arches:

These had triple, double, or a single entrance. They had no practical function but were built to commemorate significant events like military victories.

Walls:

Roman walls have many variations. The width of these walls ranges from a thin 18 centimeters to a massive six meters. They never used stone blocks or marble. Masonry walls were created out of square blocks and built without the application of mortar. They commonly utilized brick and small stones that faced a concrete core.

Conclusion

Thank you for making it through to the end of *Ancient Rome*. We hope it was informative and was able to provide you with all of the tools you needed to achieve your goals, whatever they may be.

Ancient Rome was an amazing place set amidst an interesting time. There is more to its history that we have yet to uncover. It is fun to imagine what it would have been like to live in ancient Rome. While we cannot actually be there, reading about it provides a richer experience.

With that, we have come to the end of this book. I want to thank you for choosing this book.

Now that you have come to the end of this book, we would first like to express our gratitude for choosing this particular source and taking the time to read through it. All the information here was well researched and put together in a way to help you understand the Ancient Greece as easily as possible.

We hope you found it useful and you can now use it as a guide anytime you want. You may also want to recommend it to any family or friends that you think might find it useful as well.

Finally, if you found this book useful in any way, a review is always appreciated!

Made in the USA
Monee, IL
23 October 2020